BORN
GAY

BORN GAY

THE PSYCHOBIOLOGY OF SEX ORIENTATION

**GLENN WILSON
AND QAZI RAHMAN**

PETER OWEN
LONDON AND CHESTER SPRINGS

PETER OWEN PUBLISHERS
73 Kenway Road, London SW5 ORE
First published in Great Britain by
Peter Owen Publishers 2005, reprinted 2005
This edition 2008
© Glenn Wilson and Qazi Rahman, 2005
All rights reserved.
A catalogue record for this book is available
from the British Library
ISBN 978-0-7206-1309-4
Printed and bound in the UK by CPI Bookmarque,
Croydon, CR0 4TD

CONTENTS

PREFACE 9

CHAPTER **ONE**   **Where are gays found?** 13
Who are you calling gay? *13*
Either/or *16*
The sexual lie detector *20*
Homosexuality is not common, but it is stable *22*

CHAPTER **TWO**   **The failure of psychosocial theories** 29
Psychoanalytic ideas *30*
Social learning theory *33*
The seduction hypothesis *34*
Child-rearing effects *36*
Cross-cultural comparisons *38*
Bem's alienation theory *38*
Therapy for sexuality? *40*

CHAPTER **THREE**   **Not all in the genes** 43
Family connections *43*
Genes versus environment *45*
Which genes, where? *50*
The mitochondrial DNA theory *53*
Mechanism of the genetic effect *54*

CHAPTER **FOUR**   **Is homosexuality adaptive?** 57
Kin selection *57*
Parental manipulation *59*
Balanced polymorphism *59*
The value of same-sex bonding *61*
How much can we learn from animal behaviour? *62*
A new scenario *64*

CHAPTER **FIVE**   **Hormones in the womb 69**
How hormones work *69*
Middle-sex *72*
Finger lengths *77*
Fingerprints *80*
Auditory mechanisms *82*
Do gay men have bigger penises? *84*
Physical growth *86*
Onset of puberty *88*
Maternal stress and substance use *89*
Developmental instability *92*

CHAPTER **SIX**   **The big brother effect 95**
The 'fraternal birth order effect' *95*
How many brothers does it take to make you gay? *98*
Social environment and the big brother effect – is there a link? *100*
The mother's immune system *102*
The H-Y antigen *103*

CHAPTER **SEVEN**   **The gay brain 107**
The hypothalamus *107*
Lesbianism and the limbic system *115*
Cognitive abilities *116*
Brain asymmetry *121*
Handedness and sexual orientation *123*
Conclusion *126*

CHAPTER **EIGHT**   **Childhood indications** 127
Feminine boys and masculine girls *127*
CGN, learning and prenatal factors *130*
Adult 'psychological gender' *132*
CGN and psychological health *133*

CHAPTER **NINE**   **Are there different types?** 137
Perceptions *137*
The research *138*
Sex hormone comparisons *140*
Finger-length ratios *142*
Conclusions *143*

CHAPTER **TEN**   **The science of sexual orientation and society** 145

REFERENCES 151

INDEX 171

PREFACE

ARE YOU GAY or straight? Although some people go through a phase of uncertainty, most of us have a fairly clear idea of our own preference. The next question that arises, perhaps especially if we recognize that we are gay, is how we came to be that way. Throughout history there have been many conflicting theories, including 'perverse choice', seduction by older gays, being raised by smothering mothers and absent or aloof fathers, chance conditioning, traumatic early heterosexual experiences and genetics. There have also been widely varying attitudes, ranging from tolerance and amusement to moral outrage and psychiatric classification as an 'illness'. Although psychiatry no longer regards homosexuality as a deviation or mental disorder, and equality is enshrined in law in Anglo-American countries, there are many religions around the world that regard gays as stubbornly 'sinful' people whose behaviour is an affront to the divine plan.

Searches for the causes of the homosexual orientation began in the era when the behaviour was pathologized (believed to be a disease or mental illness), hence some gay people have been resistant to the idea of science seeking answers to this question. However, since a self-declared gay neuro-scientist in San Diego found anatomical brain differences between gay and straight men, the homosexual community has come to realize that science might just as well be used to dispel the idea that gay behaviour is a matter of fickle choice subject to 'correction'. Scientific work has progressed a great deal since the ground-breaking discovery of Simon LeVay in 1991, and this book is intended to summarize these modern developments.

Our sexual orientation is a fundamental aspect of our underlying human nature. After our gender, and perhaps ethnic group, our sexual orientation is probably the next key attribute defining who one is as a human being. No wonder then that lay people and scientists alike are fascinated, and sometimes alarmed, by what makes us gay, lesbian, bisexual or straight. Modern sexual orientation research comes from many disciplines, including psychology, neuroscience, genetics, endocrinology and evolutionary biology. Together we have termed these overlapping sciences 'psychobiology', and this book sets out to communicate some of the key findings within this field. It would be naïve to say that the content of this book has no relevance to certain social issues surrounding sexual orientation, so these will be addressed as necessary.

Although work on the origins of sexuality has been sensitive from the outset, the accumulation of evidence from independent laboratories across the world has shown that the biological differences between gay and straight people cannot be ignored. Science is our best tool for seeking truth about nature even if the facts it provides are sometimes counterintuitive or discomforting. Some people may be unhappy with some of the major themes in this book, but a growing number of people around the world believe these issues are important and that research on sexual orientation is no longer taboo. So let us not beat around the bush but state our central conclusion clearly: *Modern scientific research indicates that sexual orientation is largely determined by the time of birth, partly by genetics, but more specifically by hormonal activity in the womb arising from various sources.*

Some see the science of sexual orientation as reinforcing old and damaging commonsense ideas about homosexuals, but this is not the case. The scientific approach, which tests ideas to see which survive in a kind of 'survival of the fittest ideas', show that most commonsense theories about sexual orientation are untrue. For example, there is no evidence for the notion that homosexuals can 'seduce' others into becoming gay, or that gay parents influence the sexual orientation of their biological or adopted children. Hence scientific knowledge may help to combat certain prejudices associated with diverse sexual preferences.

The book will help unravel the fundamental basis for sexual orientation in both men and women. Unlike the authors of some books, we do not ignore research on lesbians. We will show that male and female sexual orientation sometimes appear as parallel (or reflected) cases and sometimes seem to follow separate rules. We also look at differences *within* sexual orientation, that is, considering the question of whether gay men and lesbians can be meaningfully classified into subtypes like 'butch' and 'femme'. This and other research challenges the simplistic notion that gay men have female brains while lesbians have male brains. Rather, it emerges that homosexual people (like most heterosexuals) are possessed of a 'mosaic' style of brain, comprising a mixture of male and female attributes. Ultimately, we believe this book will confirm what most of us have always intuitively felt: that our sexual preference is a fundamental and immutable component of our human nature.

Glenn Wilson and Qazi Rahman

London, 2005

CHAPTER **ONE**

Where are gays found?

SEXUAL ORIENTATION REFERS to one's degree of sexual attraction to either men or women. For the most part biology dictates that men will mate with women, and women with men, but for a minority the homosexual impulse is equally compelling. The prevalence of heterosexual and homosexual orientations, and indeed bisexuality, has been the subject of much interest and argument over the years. The common view (particularly among the gay community) is that about one in ten people are more or less exclusively gay or lesbian. In reality the figure is much lower, but before we consider the question of prevalence we need to be clear as to how we define and measure sexual orientation. Another important question that is addressed in this chapter is whether sexual orientation is a 'black and white' phenomenon, or whether it is more accurate to think in terms of 'shades' of sexual preference on a spectrum ranging from heterosexual to homosexual. Finally, we consider whether it is possible to find some kind of physiological 'litmus' that can be used to assess someone's sexual orientation objectively.

Who are you calling gay?

Scientists and lay people alike have used several ways of classifying people into gay, straight, lesbian or somewhere in between (although, as we shall see, intermediate categories such as bisexuality and asexuality are relatively elusive and might not really exist at all). Among the classification criteria used are:

▶ the labels people apply to themselves (e.g. 'gay', 'lesbian', 'bisexual' or 'straight')
▶ their actual sexual behaviour (e.g. numbers of male versus female partners in the past and present)
▶ self-reported sexual feelings (e.g. fantasies and desires)

▶ genital or brain responses (physiologically measured arousal to male and female images).

These different methods for measuring sexual preferences do not always agree, which raises the question as to which are the best indicators.

The labels that people use to define themselves are often influenced by politics and cultural climate. Throughout history there have been compelling reasons for gay people to remain closeted. In many countries, especially Islamic states, homosexuality remains a capital crime. Nearer to home, consider the lawsuits involving Oscar Wilde (who was imprisoned for sodomy) and Liberace (who won damages against a British newspaper which accused him of being gay). Hollywood stars, such as Rock Hudson, have often been required to feign marriages and many still today fear loss of credibility in romantic roles if viewed as gay. The furore over the ordination of gay bishops in the Anglican Church underscores the considerable ambivalence within Christianity. Less commonly, reverse pressures have been observed. For instance, some men label themselves gay because they are engaged with an open and vibrant gay community, and some women identify themselves as lesbians in connection with feminist politics. At the height of the 'swinging' sixties and seventies 'bisexuality' became fashionable as a self-description, either because it denoted a tolerant, hippy-style, all-embracing love, or because it was a euphemism for homosexuality. When in the 1980s it was put to actor/director Simon Callow by a diffident young female television interviewer that he might be bisexual he responded with mock outrage: 'Good heavens, madam, whoever told you that? I am homosexual!' Callow was not willing to prevaricate with respect to this issue; but, clearly, self-labelling cannot be relied upon as a means of classifying sexual orientation.

People's actual sexual behaviour can also be misleading, since it is influenced by many factors unrelated to sexuality. Among these are moral or legal constraints, lack of opportunity for preferred sexual outlets (as in the navy, prison or boarding school) and financial gain (many 'rent boys' are heterosexual, and some prostitutes are lesbian). Sexologist Dr John Money illustrates the difference between act and status with what he calls the 'Skyscraper Test' (Money, 1988). A crazed, gun-toting male terrorist pushes a hapless male tourist to the edge of the Empire State Building and demands he perform oral sex on him or go over the edge. If the tourist is heterosexual, and yet obliges, we would hardly say that his sexual orientation has changed because of this act. More subtle pressures to conform with heterosexual norms sometimes push gay men and lesbians towards having sex with opposite-sex partners contrary to their real feelings. Some find it easier just to go through the motions of heterosexual behaviour than to deal with the social stigma of being called gay. Also, homosexual people are not without parental urges, and until recently it was pretty much necessary to get married in order to have children (as remains the case in most countries).

These two measures (labelling and actual sexual behaviour) correlate poorly with the other two approaches – sexual feelings and genital responses. Self-reported sexual feelings (fantasies and desires) would seem to be more closely related to what we would call a person's 'true sexuality' than actual behaviour, and for most practical purposes these provide the best approach to categorization. However, they do depend upon people being willing and able to report accurately, and this cannot always be taken for granted. For one thing, homosexual fantasies are quite common in heterosexual men and women as a form of 'mental exploration', and unless they predominate within mental life they do not usually imply repressed homosexuality. The term 'bi-curious' refers to that fact that many people who are basically straight might consider an occasional homosexual adventure simply to broaden their horizons. On the other hand, some people appear to 'protest too much'. In a famous experiment by Henry Adams and colleagues at the University of Georgia (Adams *et al.*, 1996) it was found that men who expressed hostile feelings towards homosexuals (homophobes) showed greater signs of erectile response when viewing film clips depicting homosexual activity than heterosexual men who were more accepting of homosexuality. This finding suggests that homophobia might be masking homosexual urges that are unacceptable to the self via the Freudian defence mechanism called 'reaction formation'. If that is the case, then physiological measures may be the best means of all of assessing sexual orientation. By observing genital responses (e.g. a penis volume measure for men or vaginal blood flow for women) to erotic stimuli (pictures of nude men and women and depictions of heterosexual and homosexual activity), or brain responses (by EEG or functional MRI scans), we obtain objective information regarding an individual's erotic preferences and arousal patterns. When self-reported desires and physiological responses agree there is no problem; when they provide conflicting information, the latter are perhaps more telling because they are less susceptible to social pressures or conscious impression management.

Either/or

Having established that what counts is the way people respond emotionally to sexual stimuli, rather than what they say or do, the next question that arises is whether sexual orientation is naturally categorical or continuous. In other words, do people tend to fall into one 'camp' or the other, or do most fall in between? Possible intermediate positions include asexuality (lack of interest in any kind of sex), bisexuality (attraction to both sexes equally) or the flexible capacity to switch from one kind of preference to another according to circumstances. This question is important because 'bimodality' implies that sexual orientation is set from an early age, whereas a prevalence of intermediate sexualities fits better with the argument that later learning experiences, 'chance' factors or lifestyle choices are influential.

Alfred Kinsey and colleagues at the University of Indiana were the first to examine the distribution of sexual orientation. They famously concluded that heterosexuality/homosexuality comprised a spectrum or continuum for both men and women, with large numbers of people falling in the bisexual range. The classic 'Kinsey scale', ranging from '0' for exclusive hetero- sexuality to '6' for exclusive homosexuality (with five intermediate degrees of bisexuality) is still widely used. Today, however, it is usually applied separately to questions of attraction, fantasy, behaviour and identity. (Kinsey has been criticized for unjustifiably lumping feelings and behaviour together.) When neuroscientist Simon LeVay presented the actual percent- ages from Kinsey's data for men as a bar chart (see Figure 1.1), a clear 'skew' towards heterosexuality was apparent (meaning there are many more heterosexuals than homosexuals). More important, there were also more homosexuals than bisexuals. Thus the chart looked 'bimodal', pointing to two discrete groups rather than a spectrum of sexuality. Rather than a bell- shaped curve (which is what you would get if most men were bisexual) we find a reversed J-shaped curve for sexual orientation in men, most being strongly heterosexual but a minority being equally decisively gay. Women did show more of a spectrum of sexuality, although still with a clear skew towards heterosexuality.

Figure 1.1. Kinsey distribution of sexual orientation among men and women. K0 refers to people who are exclusively heterosexual while K6 are people who are exclusively homosexual; the other ratings represent degrees of 'bisexuality' (from LeVay, 1996).

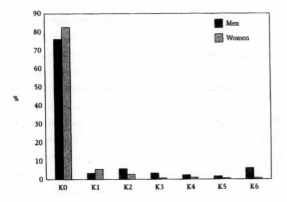

Modern studies, using more sophisticated methodology, generally confirm that Kinsey's notion of 'pan-bisexuality' is incorrect. A large-scale British survey for the period 1990–91, using around 2,000 men aged 35–44, found that 5.9 per cent had experienced some homosexual attraction and 8.4 per cent had engaged in homosexual activity at some time in the past. However, less than 1 per cent had engaged in homosexual behaviour within the preceding five years (Wellings *et al.*, 1994). Apparently, homosexual activity occurs more during adolescence, and declines with age to a more minority but exclusive state. In the overall sample, the data suggested a major skew in favour of heterosexuality with a progressive tapering off in numbers endorsing each Kinsey level of homosexual interest for women certainly, and to some extent for men. A comparable US study reported a similar pattern, again with a minority homosexual preference (Laumann *et al..*, 1994). The most recent British survey in 2000 (with over 11,000 people interviewed) found that 2.6 per cent of men and 2.6 per cent of women reported having homosexual partners in the past five years (Johnson *et al.*, 2001; Erens *et al.*, 2003). Regarding sexual attraction, the new survey revealed that 0.9 per cent of men reported only ever being attracted to the same sex, whereas 0.2 per cent of women did. There were equally few bisexual respondents (0.5 per cent for men and 0.8 per cent for women).

Interestingly, 5.3 per cent of men and 9.7 per cent of women reported being mostly attracted to the opposite sex (i.e. heterosexual) but at least once to the same sex. This reduced the percentage of exclusive heterosexuals to 91.9 per cent in men and 88.3 per cent in women. Some take this to support the bisexuality or continuum argument; others prefer to think in terms of extraneous forces resulting in an occasional lapse from primary heterosexuality.

A survey in New Zealand (Dickson *et al.*, 2003) of over 1,000 people showed that, among men at age 26, 1.2 per cent reported exclusive homosexual attraction compared with 0.2 per cent who claimed bisexual attraction. For women at age 26 there was no elevation at the homosexual end of the scale: 0.8 per cent reported exclusively homosexual attraction and 0.8 per cent bisexual attraction (see Figure 1.2). Again, in this study there was a tendency for more past homosexual activity to be reported by men (prior to the age of 26) than current activity, with a progression towards either exclusive heterosexuality or homosexuality with increasing maturity (3.5 per cent reported homosexual contact during the last 12 months compared with 8.9 per cent throughout the lifetime). This was also the case for women (3.2 per cent during the past 12 months, compared with 9.7 per cent for lifetime reporting). This is partly because all forms of sexual activity (including masturbation) tend to decline with age but also because people tend to focus progressively on what works best for them.

Figure 1.2. Distribution of sexual attraction in the New Zealand study with 485 men and 473 women (from Dickson *et al.*, 2003).

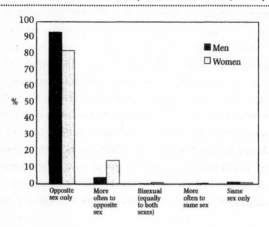

A Norwegian study (Traeen *et al.*, 2002), with a random sample of 5,000, showed negligible bisexuality in men between 18 and 49 years of age, whereas 3.3 per cent reported exclusive homosexual fantasy, attraction and romantic attachment. In women, between 0.4 per cent and just over 1 per cent reported exclusive homosexual fantasy, attraction and romantic attachment, with 0.1 per cent to 3 per cent reporting bisexuality in these categories. Behaviourally, 2.8 per cent of men reported exclusive same-sex contact, compared with 0.7 per cent of women (see Figure 1.3). The researchers in this study were unclear as to whether they were looking at lifetime experience or more recent feelings and behaviour.

Figure 1.3. Distribution of sexual attraction in the Norwegian study with 939 men and 1132 women (Traen *et al.*, 2002).

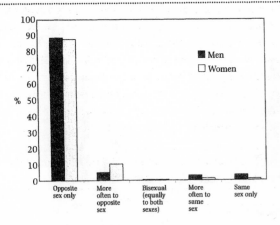

In a large representative sample of Australian twins, Mike Bailey and his colleagues found that, of around 4,700 participants, about 2 per cent reported completely homosexual feelings (fantasies and attraction), with around 0.4 per cent to 1 per cent reporting more bisexual responses, whereas in women there was no elevation at the homosexual end of the scale (Bailey *et al.*, 2000). The work of Dean Hamer and his colleagues at the National Cancer Institute in Bethesda, USA, found striking bimodality from their study of the genetics of sexual orientation (unpublished, see LeVay, 1996; see Chapter 3). They deliberately included a large number of gay men and lesbians in their study because in most studies the homosexuals get swamped by the predominance of heterosexuals. Although this approach might produce distortion as a result of recruitment avenues (gay clubs and networks), the 'saturated' sample might offer a better glimpse of the 'true' distribution. Hamer and colleagues found a clear-cut bimodality for men with respect to fantasy and attraction. In fact, some have called this the 'U-shaped' curve because almost no one fell into the 'bisexual' categories of the Kinsey scales used. That is, you are either a gay man or a straight man, and seldom in between. For women, bisexuality did emerge to some extent, but there was still a strong tendency towards bimodality (see Figure 1.4).

Figure 1.4. Distribution of sexual orientation from Dean Hamer and team, unpublished data (522 men and 892 women).

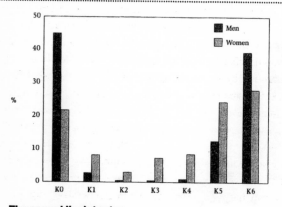

The sexual lie detector

If sexual orientation is categorical in men, but less so in women, can we see this in the sexual arousal patterns of men and women? The answer is yes. As noted above, we can measure sexual arousal in men as an increase in penis volume owing to engorgement with blood in response to pornographic imagery. This technique, called penile plethysmography, is an established measure of sexual arousal in men that is widely used for research, clinical and forensic purposes to 'diagnose' sexual targets. In women, a technique called vaginal photoplethysmography records colour changes in the walls of the vagina as it becomes engorged with blood (easier to observe accurately than clitoral erection, which might be a more precise parallel).

Heterosexual and gay men are easily differentiated on the basis of their genital responses. Homosexual men show more genital arousal to erotic stimuli depicting men than those depicting women, and the opposite is true of heterosexual men (Chivers *et al.*, in press; Freund, 1963; Freund *et al.*, 1989; Sakheim *et al.*, 1985). As we have seen, what is particularly interesting about the penile plethysmographic approach is that it provides evidence on men who wish to conceal or fabricate their true sexual preference. Despite protestations, homophobic men are more responsive to gay stimuli than heterosexual men who are relatively tolerant of homosexuality. A recent study by Mike Bailey, a leading international figure in sexual orientation research, and his team from Northwestern University in Illinois sheds much light on the question of whether bisexuality is real. They recruited 38 self-identified gay men, 33 self-identified bisexual men and 30 straight men from the Chicago area. All were shown non-sexual films, as well as two types of sexual films (some showing two men having sex with each other, and others depicting sex between two women). The reason for this is that same-sex stimuli are most effective in differentiating gay and straight men (gay men are more aroused by the gay sex film and straight men by the lesbian sex film); if they were presented with a heterosexual film, that is one in which a man and a woman are having sex, it would be difficult to tease out a sexual-orientation-related response. For example, if gay men were aroused by a heterosexual film we might erroneously conclude that they were secretly heterosexual when in fact they were aroused only by the sight of the male actor, with the presence of the female being irrelevant. As expected, Bailey and his team found that gay men and straight men showed opposite arousal patterns, favouring male and female stimuli respectively. Most interesting, however, was the finding that men who labelled themselves 'bisexual' *did not* respond to both; almost all showed the homosexual arousal pattern (although a few showed a heterosexual response). Hence, regardless of the way they classify themselves, men tend to get aroused to men only, or women only, but not to both. The remaining question is why some men view themselves, or want others to see them, as bisexual.

How about women? Does the same finding apply? Research by the same team using a similar approach (this time with heterosexual films, gay male films and lesbian films) found that the sexual arousal patterns in women (using vaginal photoplethysmography) did not differentiate between lesbian and straight women. That is, both showed a 'bisexual' pattern of genital arousal. What are we to make of this? Either bisexuality is the norm for women, or we cannot rely on genital arousal as an indicator of their sexual orientation (as we can for a man). Since there seems to be much less agreement between self-reported sexual preferences and sexual arousal, a multidimensional approach to assessment of sexual orientation in women seems to be necessary. We must bear in mind also that vaginal photoplethys-mography is not as reliable a measure of sexual arousal in women as the penile plethysmography is in men; it is not a very comfortable procedure and is affected by small movements, particularly of the pubic region. Not surprisingly, women are less willing to volunteer as subjects for research of this kind.

The conclusion from all the above research is that sexuality is fairly categorical in men but much less clearly so in women. Of course, even if it were ultimately discovered that sexual orientation is spectral rather than categorical, this would not rule out biological causation. Height is a trait that is clearly genetic but also exists on a spectrum. However, studying the biology of height (particularly its genetic basis) is made more difficult by its continuous distribution. Similarly, the biological basis of sexual orientation will be more easily understood if the indications are correct that, for men at least, it is not so much graded as an either/or phenomenon.

Homosexuality is not common, but it is stable

What, then, is the consensus about how many gay men, lesbians, hetero-sexual men and heterosexual women there are in the population? In short, no consensus exists, but from the analysis of the key work cited above we can argue that, using *feelings-based* criteria, about 2–3.5 per cent of men are completely gay, and 0.5–1.5 per cent of women are completely lesbian. This leaves around 98 per cent of people more or less completely heterosexual. Clearly the notion that around one in ten people are gay is wrong. The true figures are more like one in 30 for men being gay and one in 70 for women being lesbian (though women seem to have greater flexibility). These figures may seem surprisingly low, but gay men and lesbians still constitute a sub-stantial minority group, whose disposable income is recognized in the commercial concept of 'the pink pound' and whose electoral influence is ignored by politicians at their peril.

Since gay people gravitate towards permissive, cosmopolitan centres like London, San Francisco and Sydney, and tend to move within their own circles once there, it may be hard for them to see that they constitute a fairly small group within the population at large. For example, in London (a city of about 8 million people) the number of men reporting homosexual behaviour during the past five years is 5.5 per cent, compared with 2.1 per cent for the rest of Britain. For women the figures are 3.9 per cent in London, compared with 2.4 per cent for the rest of the UK (Johnson *et al.*, 2001). Hence there is no doubt some truth behind the character of Daffyd in the comedy TV series *Little Britain*, who covets his unique status as 'the only gay in the village'.

The prevalence of homosexuality seems to be more or less the same across cultures. Social anthropologist Frederick Whitam has done much important work on comparing the frequency and manifestation of homosexuality across different cultures. His studies spanning many years of fieldwork in the United States, Guatemala, Brazil and the Philippines, among other countries, have revealed several stable features of male homosexuality. Regardless of culture, gay men constitute no more than (and probably less than) 5 per cent of the population, and this percentage remains stable over time. Social values have minimal impact on the emergence of homosexuality, either to impede or encourage it. Given a large enough population pool, gay communities appear in all societies (Whitam, 1983) and it is only their superficial visibility that is much affected by social pressures. Whitam also conducted fieldwork on lesbian sexuality in Brazil, Peru, the Philippines and the United States and, although not looking at prevalence directly, reckoned that lesbians constituted around 1 per cent of the population in each of these cultures (Whitam *et al.*, 1998). Other aspects of homosexuality, such as the apparent femininity of gay men and tomboy tendencies of lesbian women (both in childhood reports and in adulthood), also appear as consistent across cultures.

Does this mean that sexual orientation is stable? Homosexuality has certainly been around from prehistoric times (Taylor, 1997). Historically, the most cited example of widespread homosexuality has been the Greeks of around 2,500 years ago (who were in fact comprised of diverse cultural groups). Some have argued that homosexuality was endemic and highly valued among the ancient Greeks, but this is probably an exaggeration.

Relationships mostly took the form of an older, married and socially prestigious man forming a sexual liaison with a much younger, unmarried,
adolescent boy. These relationships were mostly frowned upon, and often
families would aim to prevent their sons entering into such relationships.
There was also a kind of 'buddy system' on the battlefield whereby a senior
officer would be supported by an apprentice boy, who would 'fag' for him –
clean his boots, polish his sword and offer sexual gratification if called upon
(cf. the midshipmite in the Royal Navy). This did not necessarily mean that
either was truly homosexual; the senior soldier was again usually married
(but away from home), and rewards for valour in battle were women not
boys. Both the Greeks and the Romans differentiated between adult heterosexuals and homosexuals, suggesting that homosexuals were a 'special
class' of people, not simply heterosexuals engaging in the occasional gay
sex. In the absence of written works, historians have perhaps over-egged the
extent of homosexuality among the ancients on the basis of themes in art-
works such as paintings, statues and pottery. In fact, it is more likely that
homosexuality was over-represented among visual artists as a specific
group. Certainly, ancient texts such as the Bible and Koran are not noted for
proclaiming homosexuality as normative. Further discussion of cross-
cultural and historical aspects of homosexuality is found in Chapter 2 as
they relate to certain obsolete social acquisition theories. Suffice to say at
this point that the best guess we can make is that homosexuality has existed
throughout history to much the same degree as it does today.

What of modern work on the stability of sexual orientation? The recent
British National Survey of Sexual Attitudes and Lifestyles provides some
interesting comparisons. This study was conducted twice, once during
1990–91 (Wellings *et al.*, 1994), then again during 1999–2001 (Johnson
et al., 2001; Erens *et al.*, 2003). Comparison of the two surveys indicates
that homosexual attraction in men went up from 0.5 per cent (in the
1990–91 survey) to 0.9 per cent (in the 1999–2000 survey). In women it
went down slightly, from 0.3 per cent to 0.2 per cent. For homosexual
behaviour over the past five years, the rate in men goes from 1.5 per cent (in
1990–91 survey) to 2.6 per cent (in the 1999–2001 survey). For women, it
went up from 0.8 per cent to 2.6 per cent by the second survey. On the sur-
face this might seem like an increase in homosexuality, but there are reasons
for doubting this conclusion. For one thing, the attraction measure showed

a slight decline over time for women. It is also difficult to know whether the apparent increases result simply from people being more honest about reporting homosexual attractions and encounters (because of the more tolerant attitudes towards homosexuality which this survey also found; Copas *et al.*, 2002). The researchers themselves explored this issue using reported abortion rates as a comparison. They also took account of the attitude change towards homosexuality between surveys, as well as the methods used (paper and pencil questionnaires in the 1990–91 survey versus computer-assisted self-interview in the 1999–2000 survey). Their conclusion was that the apparent increase in homosexual behaviour was because of an increase in the candour of reporting sensitive behaviours resulting from increased social tolerance and improved methodology (Copas *et al.*, 2002). A detailed examination of the data revealed that any rise in the reporting of homosexual experience was restricted to those heterosexuals who reported being attracted to same-sex partners, or having had a same-sex encounter at least once. We have already argued that occasional exploratory and opportunist homosexual acts do not define homosexuality, nor detract from basic heterosexuality.

Other evidence for the stability of sexual orientation comes from studies of the number of people switching persuasions at various stages of life. In the New Zealand study described earlier (Dickson *et al.*, 2003), between the ages of 21 and 26 years only 1.9 per cent of men moved away from an exclusively heterosexual attraction and only 1 per cent moved towards it. In women around 9.5 per cent moved away from exclusive heterosexuality and 1.3 per cent moved towards it. Hence, if you were to track people over time you would find that almost no men move between sexual orientations, and only a small proportion of women. This constitutes further evidence that female sexuality is more flexible than men's, even though it can still be said to be reasonably stable.

This issue was further explored by Angela Pattatucci and Dean Hamer. They assessed 358 lesbian, bisexual and straight women on the ubiquitous Kinsey scales (separately for identification, attraction, fantasy and behaviour) and followed up a sub-sample 12–18 months later. Movement between sexual orientations was observed in about 20 per cent of women. Those who were more or less completely lesbian or straight in the first instance tended to stay put, with movement being confined mostly to the bisexual range of Kinsey scores.

One recent study seemed to suggest that over a quarter of lesbian/bisexual women relinquished their sexual orientation in favour of a heterosexual one over a five-year period (Diamond, 2003). This sounds a lot, but closer examination of the data fits a stability argument better than a fluidic one. The sample consisted of 80 supposedly non-heterosexual women (with no comparison group of heterosexual women), and 22 reported changes in their sexual orientation. However, of these, ten claimed they were heterosexual at year five and 12 had not labelled themselves as anything at all. Eliminating this group means that 58 out of 80 (73 per cent) of the women remained lesbian or bisexual over the five-year period, and those who did end up heterosexual reported low sexual attraction to women in the first place. Thus, fundamental changes in sexual orientation as defined by sexual feelings seem to be quite rare. Other factors related to how people interpret and act on their sexual preferences (stigma associated with a lesbian or gay identity) seem to be responsible for many apparent changes.

From all the above discussion we could argue that sexual orientation in humans is 'taxonic'. A recent taxometric analysis, using complex statistical procedures with a large Australian twin sample, has shown that the distinction between heterosexuality and homosexuality is not arbitrary, but that latent taxa underlie these preferences (Gangestad et al., 2000). Taxa are non-arbitrary classes whose existence is empirically based, rather than a simple semantic classification. The techniques of taxometry test whether statistical associations between robust correlates of proposed taxa, such as sexual orientation, show evidence of true categories. The taxonicity of sexual orientation indicates that, for men at least, a dichotomous biological pathway could account for its variation. In the following chapters we will see that a model based on hormonal influences on brain development during early life in the womb is one candidate for such a pathway driving development down a sex-typical route in the majority (heterosexual) but also down an atypical route in the minority (homosexuals).

In summary, sexual orientation (for men at least) seems to be categorical (either/or) rather than continuous (mostly consisting of various types and degrees of bisexuality). It is best assessed by asking people about their inner desires, or measuring their genital arousal to various stimuli, rather than asking them to attach a label to themselves or by documenting their behaviour. True homosexuality, so assessed, is much less common than previously thought. There is little support for the idea that a large part of the population harbour unrealized homosexual desires or feelings (although that possibility has been raised with respect to homophobic men). In modern times it may be a lot easier to accept one's homosexual feelings, but this does not mean that homosexuality has increased over time; it is just that people are more willing to be honest about it. In women, sexual orientation does seem to be more variable, with higher degrees of bisexuality being observed. This is consistent with the notion that women have greater erotic plasticity (i.e. a sex drive more open to influences of situational and cultural factors than men's: Baumeister, 2000) and suggests that male and female sexual orientation may have divergent, although overlapping, causes.

CHAPTER **TWO**

The failure of psychosocial
theories

WE ALL HAVE our own pet theories about what makes us who we
are and what makes us distinctively human. We use these for
comfort, to try and predict other people's behaviour, and to justify
our various moral and political beliefs about certain groups of people or
certain types of behaviour. In his book *The Blank Slate* (2002) psychologist
Steven Pinker talks about how we have certain tacit beliefs about human
nature and the origins of the differences between individuals. One of these is
the enduring notion that we are born as a 'blank slate' upon which experience, learning and culture 'write' our personalities and abilities (and all
other aspects of our selves, including the type of partners to whom we are
sexually attracted). Another is the equally enduring belief in a 'ghost in the
machine', the idea of a 'mind' or 'soul' that operates separately from our
body and brain. These ideas are very entrenched in modern society. We see
them everywhere we turn. For example, there is a widespread myth that
parents are responsible through their upbringing for the way their children
turn out, despite overwhelming evidence that they have minimal influence
on their children's personalities or abilities beyond that of the genes that
they pass to them (Harris, 1998). The evidence that leads to this conclusion
is detailed on page 46. There is also a popular notion that the sexes are born
identical in their dispositions and abilities, and that the differences between
men and women that are observed are down to social role learning experiences specific to 'our male-dominated society'. Human violence is frequently
put down to excessive exposure to violent role models in real life or the
media, even though the weight of evidence points to reversed cause and
effect, that innately aggressive individuals gravitate towards violent models
and images.

Such ideas have also predominated in our views of human sexuality. For
decades it was believed that gender could be 'assigned' by a conspiracy of

29

surgery and upbringing, and many boys with an XY chromosome pattern were raised as girls simply because their penises were too small or damaged. Only in recent years has the full extent of identity turmoil created by such arbitrary decisions been recognized. For a long time it has been supposed that homosexuals 'become that way' because of some kind of aberrant upbringing or seduction by older homosexuals (a Dracula-style process of initiation). Others, including many homosexuals themselves, have argued that we can 'choose' to be gay or lesbian as a matter of lifestyle choice and that we can change our sexual orientations, as if our minds were free of any constraints imposed by the wiring of our brain. (Interestingly, no one much says this about becoming straight, but then 'straightness' is generally not regarded as needing any explanation). Only now, as the modern sciences of human nature gain ground, can we appreciate that such views of the origins of human sexual orientation are just plain wrong.

Research efforts to identify psychosocial factors in the development of sexual orientation have turned up virtually nothing. In fact, the 'research' is often not actually research in the scientific sense. Psychosocial theories tend to make loose predictions about how being gay, lesbian or straight develops. For the most part they make claims that are not easily tested by the scientific method. Biological theories, on the other hand, make testable predictions about what to expect from this thing we call 'sexual orientation', generating facts that fit into broad scientific systems such as evolutionary theory.

Psychoanalytic ideas

One of the first theories to argue that we become gay or lesbian because of something aberrant in our upbringing is Sigmund Freud's psychoanalysis, a classic (if vague and all-encompassing) theory of human psychology. According to Freud, a primary driving force in human nature is our sexual drive or 'libido'. This force, perhaps conceived on the model of Victorian hydraulics, cannot be denied but can be diverted into alternative channels according to where the 'locks' direct it. Such alternatives include the direction of our sexuality. Freud argued that people go through several stages of 'psychosexual' development where the focus of eroticism (pleasure) shifts from one body part to another. As infants we gain sexual pleasure primarily from sucking our mother's nipples, or various substitutes such as 'dummies' or our thumbs (the 'oral' phase). Later on, at the time of toilet-training, children go through an 'anal phase' where pleasure is derived from defecation and the control of bowel movements. Around the age of five, boys enter an 'Oedipal phase' in which sexual urges are directed towards the mother. This 'Oedipus complex' is first 'repressed' because of fear of the father's jealousy, then ideally 'resolved' when the sexual urges are redirected to other females at puberty. Women are said to go through something broadly similar (dubbed the 'Electra complex' by Carl Jung), in which sexual urges directed towards the father (including feelings of 'penis envy') are later redirected into sexual attraction to other males.

The basic idea of psychoanalysis is that homosexual men become 'inverted' because of a failure to resolve the Oedipus complex. This, in turn, is usually attributed to an overly hostile or absent father, or an overly protective mother, or a combination of the two, although the precise mechanism is unclear. Another variation on the psychoanalytic theme is that gay men are 'stuck in', or 'regress to', a particular phase of psychosexual development, primarily the 'anal phase' or a short 'homosexual phase' which normal boys 'grow out of'. The reason why some men (and not others) fail to mature successfully remains something of a mystery but some kind of early emotional 'trauma', by now unavailable to memory or consciousness (i.e. 'repressed'), is implicated. Finally, some psychoanalysts have suggested that gay men are fearful of female genitals because of repressed fear of castration by the father, who is naturally jealous of their sexual feelings towards the mother; homosexuality thus occurs as a kind of 'displacement' of the libido towards safer territory.

There are certain claims here that can be tested to see if they are true, and on all counts they are found wanting. There is no evidence that gay men are fearful of women; in fact, gay men often feel most at home in heterosexual female company. As to whether gay men are fearful of female genitalia, the theory is unclear as to whether it is referring to an actual fear or simply an *aversion* to female genitalia. The latter would of course be expected if gay men are sexually attracted to men (and male genitals), exactly in the same way that heterosexual men are 'averse' to male genitalia without suffering any special trauma. That is, it is reasonable to expect people to show some kind of negative response, or at best indifference, to their non-preferred sexual stimuli. A distaste for bodily fluids and the genital and excretory areas of the body (with all their messy, 'dirty' connotations) may be the evolutionary norm, but one that can be powerfully overridden by sexual urges in certain circumstances. There is also scant any evidence for a truly 'homosexual phase' during development. A certain amount of same-sex horseplay is common among adolescent boys (and girls) but this occurs for a variety of reasons, usually simple proximity or availability (cf. the 'homosexuality' that is rife in prisons). Only a small proportion of boys who play adolescent games of this kind go on to become adult homosexuals.

The classic 'absent father' hypothesis (Freud, 1905) has been discounted time and time again. Although some gay men report being emotionally distant from their fathers, this is probably because of their fathers' reactions to them as gender non-conforming children (Buhrich and McConaghy, 1978; Freund and Blanchard, 1983; Isay, 1989; Ridge and Feeney, 1998). The so-called 'over-protective' mother, insofar as the idea contains any truth, may also be reacting to the perceived sensitivity of her gay son, perhaps buffering him from the father's hostility. Freudian theory would predict that boys whose fathers are physically absent from the home would be more likely to become gay, which is demonstrably not the case. Ironically, the notion of an unresolved Oedipal complex ought to apply more to heterosexual men than to gay men – after all, if gay men are fixated on their mothers (who are female), why should they fancy men?

Psychoanalytic theory is relatively unclear regarding the development of lesbianism, but generally it goes something like this: in the presence of brothers, or her father, a female will become obsessed by penis envy. She does not have a penis, but sees that male members of her family do have and, feeling some deficiency, decides she wants one too. This leads her to rebel against the female role in order to enjoy the benefits of being male, hence lesbianism. This sequence raises more questions than it answers. How do you get from rebelling against the female role to a sexual preference for women? What mechanisms are responsible for this? Why does the process occur to one woman and not the next? Does it imply that a woman with a brother is more likely to become lesbian? If so, it can be shown to be wrong.

The problem with all these Freudian-type theories is that they are often so literary and vague that there is no way they can be tested. Long ago, the philosophers of science (such as Karl Popper) reached agreement that a theory is not scientific if there is no way it can be disproved. This is the criterion of *falsifiability*. Freudian-type theories are generally not scientific because it is hard to conceive how they can be falsified. And, as we have seen above, when empirical hypotheses *are* derived from Freudian theory, they are either shown to be wrong or else a more parsimonious (obvious) explanation of the result is apparent (Eysenck and Wilson, 1973). Psychoanalysis persists in many domains of Western consciousness, especially art and literature, and is still taught to psychology students as a curiosity, or out of some misplaced nostalgia. However, it relates to scientific psychology much as astrology does to astronomy, or alchemy to chemistry. It is best regarded as a game, a party trick, like reading Tarot cards, that is beyond the pale of science.

Social learning theory

The other main approach to seeing sexual orientation as a product of psycho-social influences is that which is broadly called 'social learning' theory. This derives initially from the theories of famous behaviourists such as Ivan Pavlov, J.B. Watson and B.F. Skinner, in and around the late nineteenth and early and mid twentieth centuries. These psychologists argued, and demonstrated with considerable success, that many habits could be modified by experience or new information learned through a process called conditioning. 'Classic' conditioning refers to the discovery that if one stimulus (e.g. sight or sound) that naturally produces a particular response is repeatedly or dramatically paired with another that does not, then the latter may come to elicit that behaviour in its own right. In terms of sexual orientation (and we have all heard this one time and again) it is maintained that a person's first exciting sexual experience will determine their later sexual orientation. So, if a boy masturbates for the first time and another male hoves into view during the moment of orgasm, then the boy will have learned to associate sexual pleasure with males, thus becoming homosexual. It can also work the other way: an experience of sexual molestation by either sex might lead a person to redirect their sexual desires to the non-offending sex. (This is a favourite explanation of lesbianism, although there is no evidence that lesbians have a history of any more abuse or molestation by men than do heterosexual women.)

While the notion of conditioning has been useful for understanding the origins of certain disorders such as phobias, when it comes to sexual orientation there is little evidence to support it. A high proportion of gay men and lesbians have had heterosexual sex prior to discovering their true sexual orientation, and many heterosexuals have had their first sexual experiences with same-sex partners. For example, there is substantial same-sex activity among boys attending British public boarding schools, yet this does not increase the likelihood of homosexuality in adulthood (Wellings *et al.*, 1994). And even if gay men and lesbians do have their first sexual contacts with members of the same sex (which will be increasingly likely as society becomes more tolerant) then this is perfectly consistent with people responding according to their innate sexual orientations.

Animal models of learning also show us that conditioning may influence sexual behaviour or actual sexual performance (what we call 'consummatory' components of sexuality) but not sexual preference. For example, male rats trained to associate a smell (say lemon) with sexual activity will ejaculate more with females bearing that smell rather than females that do not carry that smell. But if you do the same, and this time present the rat with a female and male rat that both have the lemon smell, the rat will ejaculate with the female, not the male rat.

The seduction hypothesis

The idea that young boys are susceptible to initiation into the gay world by unscrupulous older males has a long history and has spawned many bizarre social policies. Some of these include the now defunct 'Clause 28' (which aimed to prohibit the 'promotion' of homosexuality in UK schools) and the higher age of sexual consent for gay men (although now no longer in UK law, many politicians still believe it was for the 'protection of children'). The seduction hypothesis comes in various forms and is the staple of learning-oriented 'therapists'. It focuses either on the notion that adolescent boys can be seduced into homosexuality by older homosexual men, or that incest between brothers in the form of childhood sex play produces a homosexual orientation (Cameron and Cameron, 1995). Several research studies show that both these hypotheses are untrue.

Khytam Dawood (of Northwestern University, Illinois) and colleagues tested the incest version of the seduction hypothesis. They wanted to see if having a gay brother was a psychosocial cause of homosexuality in men because of sex play between the brothers. The researchers examined questionnaire responses from 37 gay male sibling pairs recruited from several major metropolitan areas of the United States. Among other things the questionnaires assessed sexual orientation, sex-typed behaviours in childhood, whether they had engaged in sex play with their brothers, and if so what type of play. The gay brothers were found to be similar in some ways; for example, both brothers tended to be either more feminine or masculine in their childhood sex-typed behaviours; but the notion that gay brothers encourage the other to explore homosexuality or discover their own homosexual feelings was not supported. Participants reported that they were first aware of their homosexual feelings at around age 11, whereas they only learned of their brother's homosexuality at around age 21. Thus knowing that your brother is gay is not a powerful influence towards becoming gay. In fact, two thirds of the participants did not engage in sex play with their brothers at all, and those that did recalled earlier homosexual feelings (around age ten).

So what of the minority of men who, as boys, have had some sort of sexual activity with older boys or men? Do boys who have sex with older males become homosexual? Or is it that boys who engage in willing sexual activity with unrelated older males are acting on inborn homosexual desires? Our public views of child sexual abuse have tended to skew our view of sexual activity between children or adolescent boys and unrelated adults. Some controversial research suggests that a majority of boys (but not girls) tend to react positively (or neutrally) and show no symptoms of mental disturbance when they had willing sexual relations with unrelated older boys or adult men (Bauserman and Rind, 1997; Rind, 1998). Similarly, adolescent boys (presumably heterosexual) who have had sexual relations with adult women also tend to react positively (Condy et al., 1987). Bruce Rind (2001) from Temple University, Philadelphia, examined the responses of 26 gay men who had had age-discrepant sexual relations as adolescents between the ages of 12 and 17 years with adult males. They were found to be well adjusted in terms of self-esteem and had a positive view of their sexual identity. Almost all the men reported that they became aware of their same-sex sexual feelings, and labelled these feelings as 'gay', almost four years prior to sexual experiences with adult males, which they willingly engaged in and reported positive or neutral reactions towards.

Research such as this indicates that the seduction hypothesis is false. Some boys who are destined to become gay do indeed have same-sex sexual activity with siblings or with unrelated older males. However, the fact that the majority of men who had sex activity with either their brothers or other unrelated males knew about their own homosexual inclinations before their same-sex activities strongly suggests that childhood sex play or willing sexual activity with unrelated older males is not a cause, but rather a consequence, of inborn early homosexual feelings.

Child-rearing effects

Another source of evidence against psychosocial influences on human sexual orientation comes from studies of children raised by gay or lesbian parents. If parental influences on sexual orientation were strong, then surely having gay or lesbian parents to promote the persuasion would make the children turn out homosexual. That, however, is not the case. J. Michael Bailey and colleagues at Northwestern University (Bailey, Barbow *et al.*, 1995) recruited 55 gay men who reported on 82 sons (whom they had fathered in previous heterosexual marriages). They asked the fathers to rate the sexual orientations of their sons and posted questionnaires to the sons to ask directly their sexual orientation. The ratings showed high consistency between father and son, and of those sons who were rated with confidence, 91 per cent were heterosexual and 9 per cent were reported as gay or bisexual. Gay and heterosexual sons did not differ in other relevant variables, such as the length of time they had lived with their fathers (psychosocial theories would predict that sons who lived the longest with gay fathers would be most likely to become gay), frequency of contact with their fathers in the past year, degree of acceptance of their fathers' sexual orientation, or the quality of the father–son relationship. Although less than one in ten turns out gay, the 9 per cent homosexuality rate of sons of gay fathers is actually higher than the baseline estimates of homosexuality reported in Chapter 1. However, the methodology used in this study (recruiting gay fathers through advertisements in the gay media) is likely to have inflated the rate of homosexuality among sons because sometimes it would be the son who first registered the advertisement, directing his gay father's attention to it. The true figure is probably much lower and perhaps no different from base rates of homosexuality in the general population.

Other research, this time looking at the sexual orientation of children of lesbian mothers in the UK, concurs with the findings from Bailey's group.

Susan Golombok and Fiona Tasker of City University, London (1996), examined 25 children of lesbian mothers and a control group of 21 children of heterosexual mothers longitudinally – they were first seen at around the age of 9, and then again at around age 23. The researchers measured the sexual orientation of the young adults using a standardized interview with questions about same-sex attraction, sexual experiences, sexual identity and consideration of a lesbian or gay relationship. There were no differences between young adults raised in lesbian families and their peers from hetero-sexual mother households in same-sex attraction, and almost all young adults identified as heterosexual. Two young women from lesbian families said they were lesbians, but this does not differ significantly from controls or base rates. There was a heightened likelihood of the women raised by lesbians to have *considered* having a lesbian relationship (14 out of the 25). Some authors have confused this as indicating elevated levels of same-sex orientation but this is not really the case. Only six out of those 14 actually had same-sex contact, and this even included those with only minor contacts such as kissing someone of the same sex. As we have said, only two women reported a lasting lesbian orientation. The young adults' sexual orientations did not relate to other variables such as mothers' warmth, child's contact with the biological father, the quality of the mother's relationship with her female partner, the mother's political involvement or views of men.

Young adults raised in lesbian (or gay) families are no more likely to suffer mental health problems or have difficulties in their friendships than their peers from heterosexual homes (Golombok *et al.*, 1983; Patterson, 1992; Tasker and Golombok, 1997). These studies negate the view that childhood experience and parental treatment determine adult sexual orien-tation as well as challenging cherished beliefs about the need for fathers or male role models in making people gay, lesbian or straight. They also have social policy implications, which will be revisited in Chapter 10.

In retrospect, it is hard to see why parents should influence the sexuality of their children. The theory of 'differential reinforcement' (Ruble and Martin, 1998) proposes that parents differ in the extent to which they reinforce certain sex-typed behaviours over others. That is, some parents strongly reinforce sex-typical childhood behaviours, including heterosexuality, while others do not strongly reinforce such behaviours in their children, who may then show a greater likelihood of becoming homosexual. Thus gender socialization is conceived as a blanket process simultaneously influencing several domains of sex-related behaviour. However, recent research on twins suggests that much of the variance in childhood gender nonconformity and adult psychological gender identity is genetic (Lippa and Hershberger, 1999; Bailey *et al.*, 2000). Any remaining variance appears to be non-shared, meaning that psychosocial influences, including parental gender socialization practices, would tend to make same-sex siblings different rather than alike on sex-related traits. In any case, the causal link between strength of parental reinforcement of sex typing and sexual orientation is extremely 'noisy'.

Cross-cultural comparisons

Some classic cross-cultural evidence also discounts a role for early same-sex contacts in childhood and adolescence. The Sambia are an isolated tribe in New Guinea who culturally enforce early homosexual behaviour in boys throughout their entire adolescent period. Here we have an example of a culture that actually reinforces homosexual behaviour, much in the same way that we in the West reinforce heterosexual conduct. Sambian boys of around seven to ten are required to fellate older boys and men (in all-male houses) because the Sambia view semen as imparting health and virility. When these boys reach puberty they switch roles and initiate other younger boys into fellatio. Eventually as the boys become men and reach their young adult years they are expected to marry women and have heterosexual sex. Most have little difficulty in adapting to the role of heterosexual husband although a minority of about 5 per cent continues to engage in homosexual activity (Herdt, 1981).

In other words, despite experience of exclusive homosexual contact throughout their teenage years, Sambian males show a rate of homosexuality in adulthood that is much like that in other countries. We noted in Chapter 1 that rates of exclusive (true) homosexuality appear to be remarkably consistent across time and culture, despite radically different degrees of social approval or opprobrium.

Bem's alienation theory

Daryl Bem proposed a new theory of psychosocial influences on sexual orientation in a paper published in 1996. Bem suggested that alienation from same-sex peers (owing to a gender non-conforming temperament during childhood) was responsible for homosexual orientation. His argument was that social alienation leads the child to view same-sex peers as 'exotic' or different, and this difference is eroticized during puberty by a general arousal mechanism. Peplau and colleagues (1998) note that this theory has more difficulty in explaining lesbianism because childhood gender non-conformity by girls is much less alienating (tomboyish behaviour is more socially acceptable for girls than is the 'sissy-boy syndrome' in boys). Having older brothers may increase the feeling of difference from other males (thus accommodating the 'big brother effect' to be discussed in Chapter 6), but the theory would also predict a sororal birth-order effect for homosexual women – they should have more older sisters than heterosexual women, which is not the case. Interestingly, no postnatal theory has, as yet, adequately explained the fraternal birth order effect in homosexual men (reviewed in Blanchard, 1997; 2004). The pathway from childhood temperament, to childhood friendship patterns, to opposite-sex similarity–dissimilarity, to adult sexual orientation is also unspecified. Once again, we are not told why it should affect one child and not another. Nor does the theory specify which sex-related domain in childhood is the most important predictor. Although Bem focuses on childhood aggressiveness and rough-and-tumble play, his theory ignores other sex-typed interests (such as toy preferences) that could also influence children's playmate preferences.

The notion of non-specific arousal to a perceived exotic or novel partner implies a great deal of plasticity in the neurophysiological circuitry responsible for human sexual preferences. It is unlikely that sexual preferences are left to a general arousal mechanism during development because they are far too important in evolutionary terms to be at the whim of an accidental experience of excitement without giving some bounds to its scope or reference. At the very least, a domain-specific mechanism should account for male sexuality, which appears to be more rigid than female sexuality (Baumeister, 2000). Moreover, it seems that sexual-arousal-related neural circuitry is comprised of components that are independent of other arousal systems (Rosen and Beck, 1988; Everitt, 1990; Howard, 1995). Overall, then, Bem's theory is less than convincing and has little support.

Therapy for sexuality?

An implication of most psychosocial theories of sexual orientation is that homosexuals might be able to change their sexual orientation to hetero-sexuality through therapy. The 'aversion therapy' approach, much vaunted around the 1960s, shortly before homosexuality was legalized in Britain, is now discredited as unethical and cruel as well as ineffective in altering sexual orientation (however much it might trample homosexual urges). However, a recent study that attracted a lot of media attention and controversy claimed that a procedure more akin to psychoanalytic 'talk' therapy might be effective.

In 2003 Professor Robert Spitzer from Columbia University (New York) published a report claiming that some gay men and lesbians who under-went 'reparative therapy' (a laden term which implies that homosexuality is something to be 'repaired' back to a state of heterosexuality) reported becoming predominantly heterosexual. The study recruited 200 partici-pants (143 males, 57 females), self-selected mostly from religious organizations or political lobby groups who provide 'therapy' with the specific aim of turning gays into straights. Almost all the participants were highly religious (81 per cent were Protestant), over a third reported they had had serious thoughts of suicide related to their homosexuality, and 78 per cent reported having spoken publicly in favour of efforts to change homo-sexuality. Sexual orientation was assessed by telephone interview over a range of components such as identity, behaviour and attraction. In the media, figures of change to heterosexuality were reported as between 40 per cent and 60 per cent of the sample. In fact only 11 per cent of the males and 37 per cent of the females reported a complete change to heterosexuality.

Those figures might still seem impressive, but there are several problems with this study. First, the type of therapy used, and the principle on which it was supposed to operate, were not fully described. Nor can we be sure that the gay men and lesbians really did change their sexual orientation follow-ing reparative therapy. No physiological measurements that might detect deception, deliberate or unconscious, were reported. Some gay men and lesbians may have deluded themselves or sought to persuade others that they had changed their orientation because they had a vested interest in doing so. Clearly, this was not a representative sample of gay men and lesbians; the self-selection criteria would have resulted in a group of volunteers who were decidedly invested in showing the benefits of reparative therapy. Volunteers were recruited through so-called 'ex-gay' ministries, therapists and political organizations that promote just the sort of bias that scientific research tries to eliminate. In fact, volunteers were not included in the study unless they had demonstrated some change persisting for around five years. Not surprisingly Spitzer found the greatest changes in those components of sexual orientation that can be controlled (behaviour and identity) rather than 'core' measures of sexual orientation (attraction and fantasy). Altogether, these findings are seriously compromised and of little scientific or clinical value.

Unfortunately, many unhappy gay men and lesbians approach, or are coerced into approaching, 'therapists' for help in changing their sexual orientation. Many of the techniques applied are draconian, to say the least, and there is no real evidence that they work. Spitzer's study suffers seriously from volunteer bias and probably at best achieved some degree of self-control rather than any fundamental change in desire. The sexual orientation of gay men and lesbians (and for that matter straight men and women) in the population at large cannot be reversed by psychoanalysis, learning or heterosexual experiences. As Pinker states: 'Some parts of the mind just aren't plastic' (Pinker, 2002, p. 94). A true test of the idea would be see if heterosexual men and women can change their sexual orientations, although it is hard to imagine this being done. It would not be easy to find heterosexual persons so distraught with their sexual orientation that they would seek help to become gay or lesbian. Those gay men and lesbians who claim (and indeed believe they have achieved) a 'sexual orientation change' probably do so not because of a true change in desire but because of substantial social pressure.

The fact that heterosexuality is enshrined at just about every level in society, from images and portrayals in the media, to everyday social interactions, right up to social institutions such as marriage, would itself tend to suppress manifestations of homosexuality. In fact the sheer persistence of the homosexual orientation could be taken as *de facto* evidence of its biological determination. The social forces stacked against it are such that it is unlikely to be learned in any ordinary sense of the term.

An interesting parallel can be seen in the case of left-handedness, which is another minority persuasion that we now recognize as innate. Around the late 1940s and early 1950s, at the height of the behaviourist influence on education, many schools in Anglo-American countries adopted a policy of trying to convert 'cack-handed' writers to right-handed use of the pencil. This was often brutally enforced by corporal punishment of the offending hand. The theory was that left-handed children had accidentally started writing with the wrong hand and that early correction was necessary. After creating much anguish and confusion in these unfortunate children (whose brain wiring was almost certainly responsible for their 'aberration') the experiment ultimately failed and was abandoned. Despite a gradual shift towards recognition of the naturalness of variations in sexual orientation, remnants of a similar 'experiment' with respect to homosexual men and women continue in many countries today.

CHAPTER **THREE**
Not all in the genes

THE SEARCH FOR a 'gay gene' is one of the most controversial issues in the psychobiology of sexuality. For some, who like to think they choose their preferences 'freely', the very idea is anathema because it implies determinism. This is a misunderstanding, because without lawful cause and effect scientific enquiry would be impossible, and we are surely just as firmly pushed by our environment as by our genes. Others are receptive to the genetic view because they presume this is synonymous with biological causation. This is also a misunderstanding because environmental causes can also be biological (e.g. a bump on the head or a recreational drug). As we shall see, the issue of genes versus environment is not the same as biological versus social.

Does being gay, lesbian or straight run in families? If so, how much of this is down to genes and how much to a shared environment? If sexual orientation is to some extent an effect of genes, then which genes are involved, and where are they located within the chromosomes? What is the mechanism whereby genes push an individual towards being gay, lesbian or straight? These are the key questions addressed in this chapter (although the last of these will be taken up in greater depth later in the book).

Family connections

The first hint of an inherited component to sexual orientation comes from the fact that it tends to aggregate in families, or at least among siblings. Gay men do tend to have more gay brothers and lesbians do tend to have more lesbian sisters than their heterosexual counterparts, although the percentages vary from study to study, those that are better conducted tending to report lower rates of 'familiality'. In an early study on this topic, Richard Pillard (a psychiatrist from Boston University and James Weinrich (from the University of California in San Diego) examined a sample of 50 straight and

51 gay men. They asked these men about the sexual orientation of their siblings (115 sisters and 123 brothers) and then asked the siblings themselves by posting them sexual orientation questionnaires, telephoning them or conducting face-to-face interviews. They found that the rate of homosexuality in the brothers of straight men was about 4 per cent, consistent with base rates for homosexuality in the general population, but around 22 per cent among the brothers of gay men (Pillard and Weinrich, 1986). More recent studies find that gay men (including those who say they are bisexual) probably have between two and five times as many gay brothers as do straight men (the median rate being about 9 per cent), whereas the rate of homosexuality in the brothers of straight men is no greater than the rate in the population at large (reviewed in Pillard and Bailey, 1998). The most carefully conducted study, in which the researchers chose participants in such a way that they would not self-select themselves on the basis of their sexual orientation, reported a rate of 7–10 per cent of homosexuality in the brothers of gay (or bisexual) men who had a high degree of confidence in the accuracy of their judgements of their brothers' sexuality (Bailey *et al.*, 1999).

Although lesbian women tend to have more lesbian sisters, the findings vary a lot, ranging from a 6 per cent to a 25 per cent rate of lesbianism in sisters, compared to about 2 per cent to 10 per cent in the sisters of straight women (Bailey and Benishay, 1993; Pattatucci and Hamer, 1995). Pattatucci and Hamer reported that about a third of the daughters of lesbian (and bisexual) women were 'non-heterosexual'. Although this has yet to be replicated (and the study relied on participants' reports about their daughters) it ties in with the research discussed in Chapter 2 on the slightly elevated rates of homosexuality in the biological children of lesbian parents. There is also a small but elevated rate of homosexuality in the brothers of lesbians and the sisters of gay men, but this varies widely (Pillard and Bailey, 1998).

Of course there are many traits that also run in families where it would seem likely that the environment would play a major part (e.g. whether one is Catholic or Prostestant, or votes Labour or Conservative). There are other problems also. Some of these studies asked participants to rate their siblings' sexual orientation rather than going to the sibling directly, which could well introduce some error. For example, Mike Bailey and colleagues in Australia examined a sample from the Australian Twin Registry and found that the agreement between twins' rating of their own sexual orientation and that of their co-twins was lower than had been previously thought (Kirk *et al.*, 1999). However, the point to remember is that homosexuality does bunch together in families over and above the base rates for homosexuality in the general population. If it did not, we would really have to stop the genetic search immediately, as familial aggregation is an important prerequisite for a trait being genetically influenced. But how can we decide how much of the 'familiality' in sexual orientation is down to genes and how much is down to the fact that families tend to share quite a lot of their experiences?

Genes versus environment

If you want to separate the effects of genes from the effects of the environment, it is necessary to look to the staple research methods of the discipline known as behavioural genetics: pairs of identical or monozygotic (MZ) twins and fraternal or dizygotic (DZ) twins. These give us a useful model of genetic and environmental effects: MZ twins share 100 per cent of their genetic make-up and usually a good deal of environment, whereas fraternal twins share, on average, 50 per cent of their genes (the same as ordinary siblings) and a similar proportion of their environment. Generally speaking, closer similarities (or concordance) in a trait between MZ twins compared to DZ twins implies a greater role for genetics in that trait, because the genetic contribution between these two sets of twins differs markedly while their environment is held constant.

Another interesting group is that of adopted siblings. These are biologically unrelated to their siblings but share the same home environment. If the environment were important, adoptive siblings would be more like each other than randomly paired individuals. If genes were important, they would be more like their biological siblings, even though raised in separate homes. A key comparison, although it is often hard to find sufficient numbers to study, is that between MZ twins reared together and those reared apart in separate homes. Theories focusing on the social environment predict that those reared separately should show greater differences than those reared in the same home.

In nearly all human behavioural traits that have been studied, a substantial proportion of the variance seems to be genetically determined. In the case of intelligence and abilities it is something like 70 per cent down to the genes; for personality traits, psychiatric disorders and social attitudes it is usually more in the region of 50 per cent. This means that roughly half of the variation in a trait (e.g. the extent to which you are extrovert or intro-vert, stable or neurotic) can be attributed to genetic forces (usually the concerted effects of many different genes) and half to various aspects of the environment.

If 50 per cent of a trait is genetic, this means that the environment also plays an important role; but which particular aspects of the environment are influential? This remains something of a mystery. However, modern behavioural genetic methods are capable of dividing the variance not just into genetic versus environmental, but of dividing the environment into two major types: shared versus non-shared. Shared environmental effects refer to those forces that might be expected to make you more like your sib-lings and other members of your family with whom you have been raised. For example, if father is a punitive martinet, or mother a prostitute, this should affect your siblings as well as yourself. Geographical location, poverty versus wealth, and type of schooling are also normally shared by family members. Non-shared environmental effects are those that would make you different from other family members (e.g. birth order, peer influ-ences, accidents and illnesses that occur uniquely to you, and your mother smoking heavily during your pregnancy but not that of your siblings). The big surprise (and disappointment to both Freudian and social learning theorists) is that, especially as regards personality, there is virtually no evi-dence for shared family effects. The environmental effects that do contribute to personality are of the non-shared variety. In other words, insofar as your parents affect your behaviour they do so largely by the genes they pass on to you, not by the way they raise you.

What, then, is the situation with respect to sexual orientation? Twin stud-ies on human sexual orientation also point to the conclusion that genetics are important as well as the non-shared environment. For some time it has been recognized that MZ twins are more often concordant for homosexuality than fraternal twins. In the early days of this research some researchers came up with extraordinary, and frankly erroneous, concordances for homo-sexuality between identical twins. Franz Kallmann (1952) found the concordance for MZ twins to be 100 per cent (compared with 10 per cent for fraternal twins), but this is now known to be a gross overestimate.

Kallmann's figures were unreliable for several reasons; for example, his reliance on clinical subjects and an inability to determine whether the twins were actually genetically identical.

More recent research on the genetics of sexual orientation conducted by Mike Bailey and his colleagues paints a more complex picture. In their first study, published in the prestigious journal *Archives of General Psychiatry* (1991), Bailey travelled around several states of the US recruiting gay twins (both identical and fraternal) and adoptive brothers through gay publications and interviewing them about their sexual orientation, among other things. Bailey (and the Boston psychiatrist Richard Pillard) found that the rate of homosexuality in the brothers of gay men was 52 per cent for identical twins (that was 29 out of 56), 22 per cent for fraternal twins (12 out of 54) and 11 per cent for adoptive brothers (6 out of 57). In a later study Bailey and Bell (1993) also examined women. They recruited lesbians and their twins through adverts in lesbian publications across several US states and found that the rate of lesbianism was 48 per cent in identical twins (34 out of 71), 16 per cent in fraternal co-twins (6 out of 37) and 6 per cent in adoptive sisters (2 out of 35).

In 1993, at the same time Bailey's study on women was published, Frederick Whitam of Arizona State University and his colleagues at the University of Hawaii solicited twin pairs in which at least one twin said they were homosexual. They were asked about their sexual orientations by postal questionnaires and some by interview. These researchers reported a high concordance rate for homosexuality of just over 65 per cent in 34 male twin pairs and four female pairs, and 30 per cent for 23 pairs of fraternal twins (Whitam *et al.*, 1993). This study also managed to get hold of three sets of triplets. One set consisted of a pair of identical brothers who were both homosexual and one sister who was heterosexual. The second set consisted of a pair of identical sisters who were both lesbian and one (fraternal) sister who was heterosexual. The third set consisted of three identical brothers who were all gay.

These rates are impressive, but they do not tell us much about the *magnitude* of the genetic influence. We can use complex mathematical modelling techniques to estimate the actual heritability and also take into account things like volunteer biases (the extent to which the recruitment of gay subjects through gay/lesbian publications inflates concordance rates) and the base rate for homosexuality in the general population. Mike Bailey calculated the heritability as between 31 per cent and 74 per cent for the study with men, and 50 per cent or above for the study with women. These studies were the first really powerful evidence that a considerable part of the variation in sexual orientation can be traced to the genes.

A key problem with many of these studies is that they suffer from something called ascertainment bias. That is, gay and lesbian subjects are usually recruited through gay and lesbian publications and word of mouth (gay people recruiting other gay friends). It is possible that people recruited in this way differ in some way from gay siblings in the general population. Perhaps gay twins are more likely to be comfortable with their sexualities, more open and active in the gay community and more willing to participate in sexual orientation research. This would tend to inflate the estimates of heritability that we make. As much as we can try to control for this mathematically, it is always best to try to eliminate this confounding factor in the first place. More recent twin studies have aimed to get round this problem by starting from general-population-based volunteer twin registries (these twins one hopes being more representative of the population at large) combined with complex mathematical modelling which allows a more exact estimate, or slicing up, of the sources of variance. The disadvantage of such an approach is that very large samples are required because only a small minority will be homosexual (as we know from the data in Chapter 1).

One of the largest such studies was that of Mike Bailey and colleagues from the Queensland Institute of Medical Research, who recruited around 4,500 twins from the Australian Twin Registry (Bailey *et al.* 2000). All of them were asked to complete various measures of sexual orientation, including attraction, fantasies, behaviour, childhood sex-typical or atypical behaviour and gender identity. Concordance rates between identical twins were around 30 per cent for both males and females, much lower than previous studies. In a separate report based on the Australian data, which examined both behavioural and psychological components of sexual orientation, Kirk *et al.* (2000) estimated that the heritability of homosexuality for women is around 50–60 per cent, higher than that for men (around 30 per cent). Both reports found that the environmental component in sexual orientation was from non-shared sources, that is factors making the twins different from each other (which is consistent with the behavioural genetic findings with respect to personality mentioned above).

Bailey and colleagues (2000) also found significant heritability for child-hood gender nonconformity (CGN) for both men and women. CGN is the extent to which people choose toys and playmates and engage in childhood play activities that are more characteristic of the opposite sex. As we shall see in Chapter 8, CGN is a good predictor of adult sexual orientation. Bailey *et al.* argue that CGN may be an endophenotype, a marker for sexual orient-ation that is 'closer to the genes' than homosexual behaviour itself and easier to detect because of its more continuous (bell-shaped as opposed to bimodal) variation. Perhaps being gay, lesbian or straight is an indirect effect of genes for CGN rather than genes for sexual orientation *per se*. This question is not yet resolved.

Kenneth Kendler and colleagues from the Medical College of Virginia reported on a sample of almost 3,000 individuals and found that the rate of 'non-heterosexual orientation' (they lumped bisexual responders in with true homosexuals) among identical twins was 30 per cent, compared to 8 per cent for fraternal twins (Kendler *et al.*, 2000). Both the Australian and US studies considered the possibility that identical twins might be higher in con-cordance for sexual orientation because their parental treatment and home environment are more similar than those of fraternal twins. In other words, they questioned what is known as the 'equal environments assumption'. This is a reasonable precaution given that parents often report treating their identical twin children more similarly than fraternal twins or, indeed, ordinary (non-twin) siblings. However, this does not seem to be the case as viewed by the twins themselves. In neither the Australian nor the US studies did identical twins concordant for sexual orientation report greater similarity in their childhood experiences than identical twins that were non-concordant. In fact, in the Australian study male concordant identical pairs reported having *less* similar childhoods than the non-concordant identical pairs.

Clearly, genetic factors are involved in the origins of sexual orientation. The remaining non-genetic variance in twin studies suggests an equally important role for environmental factors, but these do not conform to the psychosocial factors assumed by Freudian and social learning theorists. As we showed in Chapter 2, Khytam Dawood and colleagues failed to find any influence of shared social factors among gay brothers typically proposed by 'contagion' theories, such as an increased amount of childhood sex play among brothers. The environmental factors that do influence sexuality seem to be primarily of a non-shared nature. Therefore they could easily include purely physical effects, such as prenatal hormone fluctuations at critical phases of brain development. Indeed, this would make sense, since it would suggest a vehicle whereby the genetic effect might operate. In other words, both the genetic and environmental effects on sexuality could be mediated by similar sex hormone variations occurring during pregnancy.

Which genes, where?

Now that we know that 'gay genes' really do exist, how do we go about finding them? Where are they located on the genome? The first clue to a genetic basis for sexual orientation comes from its bimodal nature. Then we have seen that the trait is familial, with a substantial portion of the family links being the result of shared genes. The next stage in narrowing down the search for gay genes is to explore the family pedigrees of individuals with lots of gay or lesbian members. By using a 'saturated' sample we might increase our chances of finding candidate genes.

Dean Hamer and colleagues from the National Institutes of Health in the US carried out the first molecular genetic studies of human sexual orientation (Hamer *et al.*, 1993). They carefully inspected the family pedigrees of 76 gay men and found that 13.5 per cent of the gay men's brothers were also gay (consistent with previous familial studies – this is about six times the base rate). Strikingly, Hamer and colleagues found that only two other groups of relatives had significantly higher rates of homosexuality compared to base rates: gay men were found to have more gay uncles and gay cousins (both around 7 per cent) on the mother's side of the family. No increase in gay relatives was observed on the father's side of the family. This finding was interesting because it implied that the site for the 'gay genes' might be on the X chromosome, which is passed on to a boy only by his mother. In a further test, Hamer *et al.* recruited 38 families in which there were two gay brothers (in order to 'saturate' the sample with families likely to carry gay genes) and found even higher estimates of homosexuality in maternal uncles (10.3 per cent compared with 1.5 per cent of paternal uncles) and sons of maternal aunts (12.9 per cent compared to 0 per cent of maternal uncles' sons, 0 per cent of paternal aunts' sons and 5.4 per cent of paternal uncles' sons). Another study conducted on 182 families with two or more gay brothers also found maternal transmission: around 13 per cent of the maternal uncles were gay compared to 6 per cent of paternal uncles (Sanders *et al.*, 1998).

Against these findings must be put two studies that show no such maternal line effect. Mike Bailey and colleagues recruited three different samples of gay men: one from an HIV medical centre, the second from a Chicago Gay Parade, and the third from advertisements in the gay press asking for men with gay brothers. They found no evidence of a preponderance of gay relatives in the maternal line (Bailey *et al.*, 1999). Bailey's study is noteworthy because his samples were larger than Hamer's and they also aimed to circumvent ascertainment biases. McKnight and Malcolm (2000) recruited 60 gay men and 60 straight men in Sydney, Australia, and found that although gay men reported having more gay relatives (consistent with familiality) the overall ratio of paternal-line to maternal-line homosexual relatives was identical (18:18). There was no evidence of increased homosexuality in the sons of maternal aunts compared to the sons of maternal uncles (12:12).

Critics of Hamer's discovery of an excess of gay relatives on the female side of the family say that it could be an artefact of greater familiarity and contact with the mother's relatives than those of the father. After all, a certain proportion of people have no contact at all with their father's family, and indeed may not even know who their father is. Increased rates of gay maternal relatives might also appear because of the decreased rates of reproduction among gay men. A gay gene is unlikely to be inherited from a gay father because a gay man is unlikely to have children (Risch *et al.*, 1993). At this stage it is difficult to know what to make of the conflicting findings concerning Hamer's observations.

The picture for female sexual orientation is more complex. Studies report rates of non-heterosexuality (a broader term that recognizes bisexuality in female populations) being elevated in lesbian women's sisters, daughters, nieces and female cousins through the paternal line (Pattatucci and Hamer, 1995). The pattern could fit X-linkage, but whether this is maternally or paternally derived is difficult to establish. For example, low penetrance of such genes (i.e. a lack of effect on behaviour) could mask the signs of father-to-daughter transmission. Moreover, lesbians tend to have more biological children than do gay men, which might make detection of X-linkage more difficult in females. Pattatucci and Hamer suggest that a non-sex-related chromosome (an autosome but one that is sex-limited), with lower penetrance, could also account for the familial aggregation observed.

Amidst the confusion about X-linkage of genes for sexual orientation, Hamer and colleagues conducted an analysis of the DNA of a selected group of 40 pairs of gay brothers and examined 22 DNA markers on the X chromosome. They found that 33 of the 40 gay pairs (82 per cent) shared a region of the X chromosome called q28 (hence Xq28). To confirm the significance of this finding, Hamer and his team recruited a new sample of 32 pairs of gay brothers (completely unrelated to the sample in the 1993 paper), 36 pairs of lesbian sisters and the heterosexual brothers of gay pairs (Hu *et al.*, 1995). They found that 67 per cent of gay brothers shared markers in the Xq28 region whereas none of the lesbian sisters did. The heterosexual brothers of the gay sib pairs had a 22 per cent chance of carrying the same Xq28 markers (less than the 50 per cent overlap expected by chance). This suggests that genes in the Xq28 region influence the sexual orientation of men but not women. The report by Sanders and colleagues (1998) also found 66 per cent Xq28 marker sharing in 54 pairs of gay brothers.

One failure to confirm the Xq28 effect has been reported. George Rice and colleagues from the University of Western Ontario and Stanford Medical School (Rice *et al.*, 1999) examined the DNA of 52 Canadian gay male sibling pairs and found that only 46 per cent shared Xq28 genes, which is actually below chance. There are some problems with this study that make the lack of replication less meaningful. The authors did not select families who displayed the maternal transmission reported by Hamer and his team. Thus, without 'saturating' the sample to make it easier to find the genes, they decreased their chances of finding X-linkage. Nor did they have any clear defining criteria for sexual orientation. Assessment of homosexuality depended on the investigator's subjective judgement rather than standard measures of attraction, fantasy, self-identification and behaviour. Hamer (1999) decided that the studies so far mentioned had pretty modest sample sizes and so combined all the data sets (including the negative finding of Rice and colleagues). This 'meta-analysis' yielded a figure of 64 per cent of gay brothers sharing alleles (showing the same variants of the gene) at the Xq28 region.

The lack of a consistent maternal-line effect suggests that we need to consider other patterns of genetic transmission apart from Xq28. 'Auto-somal' transmission refers to the idea of the relevant gay genes being located on chromosomes that have little to do with sexual differentiation (those other than the X/Y 'sex' chromosomes). Perhaps only families that have lots of gay members show Xq28 linkage. This complexity implies that human homosexuality is probably not down to one or two particular genes; more likely there are dozens of gay genes; that is, human sexual orientation is polygenetic. Although the completion of the Human Genome Project will provide us with new avenues for research, homosexuality is relatively rare and each 'gay gene' might exert only a small effect, hence their locations will no doubt continue to elude researchers for some time.

The mitochondrial DNA theory

In a book called *Adam's Curse* (2003) Bryan Sykes, a professor of human genetics at Oxford University, has proposed the intriguing idea that the inheritance of homosexuality might be via mitochondrial DNA (mDNA). The mitochondria are thread-like particles in the cell plasma outside of the nucleus which contains the chromosomes. While their function is mostly concerned with respiration, they also contain genetic material that is of considerable interest. mDNA is 'female' in that it passes through eggs, not sperm. A mother gives it to all her children, but only her daughters pass it on to the next generation. Apparently it is a 'selfish' DNA that would prefer a female-only species, and Sykes's idea is that male homosexuality might be an example of mDNA sabotaging masculinity. A woman's mDNA would ideally eliminate all male foetuses, but failing that might seek to 'disable' them reproductively. Of course the mDNA could not have fully succeeded in these aims or humanity would be extinct, but such a genetic sex-war scenario is conceivable. A beehive contains sterile males who work for the queen, and Sykes wondered if there could be some human parallel. If a gay son helped his mother to bring up his sisters this would benefit her mDNA.

Testing this theory is not easy. Sykes notes that it might account for the continued appearance of the gay orientation despite its more obvious repro-ductive disadvantage. It would also account for the maternal transmission observed by Hamer without recourse to X-linkage. Sykes looked to see if gay men had more sisters than brothers, but this did not seem to be the case.

However, he did note that the mothers themselves had more sisters than brothers (209 versus 132 in a survey of the mothers of 500 gay men). In other words, the gay men had far more aunts than uncles. Sykes suggests that the missing brothers may have been eliminated in the womb, whereas these mothers could only neutralize their sons by steering them towards homosexuality. Unfortunately, he did not collect data on male versus female mortality in childhood or later in life. Sykes's theory is both new and controversial, and it will be interesting to see whether evidence for it develops over the next few years.

Mechanism of the genetic effect

How exactly might gay genes make people gay? Clearly, the proteins that make up genes do not literally spell out 'gay', 'lesbian' or 'straight'. They must exert their effect by affecting brain development in some way. This is likely to be a consequence of a complex cascade of molecular events in which gay genes switch on (and off) other genes which make different proteins, which feed back into the system to switch other genes on or off. It is reasonable to suppose that any genetic contributions to human sexual orientation affect the pathways that make male brains and female brains different from one another. The X chromosome has an abundance of other genes that are known to influence sexual development (Saifi and Chandra, 1999), thus if sexual orientation were truly X-linked we would expect these genes to affect sex-typical and sex-atypical brain development and behaviour. The finding of CGN linkage with homosexuality is therefore consistent with the suspicion of X-linkage.

In Chapter 5 we discuss the specific idea of brain sexual development that is under the control of sex hormones. Briefly, sex hormone molecules (especially androgens, such as testosterone in males and oestrogens in females) influence the way the brain develops so that it becomes either male-like or female-like. These are steroids that attach themselves to receptors (like keys fitting particular locks) in certain parts of the brain that are involved, among other things, with sexual target preferences. Sex hormones influence how these parts of the brain develop, grow and link to other structures in the brain. If, for argument's sake, you have a high number of receptors for androgens in the part of the brain which controls sexual desire and motivation (e.g. particular cells in the hypothalamus) then that part of the brain may become more male-like, and you will be heterosexual. If you have fewer androgen receptors in the hypothalamus, perhaps your brain is less male-like (and more female-like) and you become gay. Now this is a very simple model, and in Chapter 7 we discuss how matters are probably much more complex. However, the number of androgen receptors you have might well depend on the activity of the gene which codes for the androgen receptor, that is the androgen receptor gene.

Not surprisingly, the androgen receptor gene was one of the first candidates to be investigated for links with sexual orientation. Jennifer P. Macke from Johns Hopkins University, Dean Hamer and team investigated the androgen receptor gene in 197 gay men and 213 subjects presumed straight (some females), and 20 pairs of gay brothers (Macke *et al.*, 1993). The researchers used biological techniques to screen the whole androgen receptor region for variation or any mutations. They found no differences between heterosexuals and homosexuals in the androgen receptor gene, and gay brothers did not share an excess of androgen receptor alleles. Hamer's team have also screened another hormone-related gene, this time a gene that allows an enzyme called aromatase to convert androgens to oestrogens within the male brain (which paradoxically is one of the normal pathways through which testosterone exerts its masculinizing effect). They found no differences in these genes between homosexuals and heterosexuals either (DuPree *et al.*, 2004). Currently studies are under way scanning the entire genome for sexual-orientation-related genes. No doubt these will eventually reveal several genes influencing sexuality.

A common misunderstanding we often hear when discussing genetic research on sexual orientation is 'It's all genetic then?' Steven Pinker points this out as an oddity in current thinking among many academics and lay people alike: people all of a sudden lose their ability to distinguish 50 per cent from 100 per cent (Pinker, 2002). So far we have shown that, although genetic factors are important in sexual orientation, genes do not account for everything. Less than half the variation in sexual orientation can be ascribed to genetic differences between individuals. The rest is therefore down to environment, which everyone assumes means nurture (another oddity in modern intellectual thought driven by the blank slate notion). Yet we have also shown (in Chapter 2) that how your parents raised you, your social environment and learning, exert no measurable effect on whether you turn out to be gay, lesbian or straight. So what type of environment is as important as genetics? In Chapters 5 and 6 we aim to show that it is a non-social type of environment that is important, in particular the prenatal environment of the womb. But in the next chapter we digress slightly to consider some questions about the ultimate origins of homosexuality.

CHAPTER **FOUR**
Is homosexuality adaptive?

ONE OF THE big mysteries about homosexuality, especially given its genetic component, is how it has survived in the face of evolutionary forces. After all, homosexuals have fewer children than heterosexuals – gay men have around one fifth to one tenth the number of children as heterosexual men (Bell and Weinberg, 1978; Hamer and Copeland, 1994), and something similar probably applies to lesbian women. Surely the process of evolution would select against 'gay genes' and ultimately eliminate them?

Some people, among scientists and public alike, use this argument as a reason why homosexuality could not be biological. However, this displays a poor understanding of evolutionary biology. Genes for a particular physical or behavioural trait persist because that trait is an 'adaptation' (or a 'design') that solved a particular problem prevailing at some phase of evolution. This problem may be an ongoing one or one that our ancestors faced millennia ago. A successful design will increase the genes for itself and increase their numbers within the gene pool. Being sexually attracted to the opposite sex is a particularly useful adaptation because it prompts you to produce lots of offspring and this is why genes for heterosexuality dominate the planet. But since genes promoting homosexuality also seem to exist, it is likely that they serve, or once served, some reproductive value to themselves. We have already seen in the mitochondrial DNA theory one possible argument – the female line might benefit from non-reproductive males who assist in the survival of their sisters. But this is only one of several evolutionary scenarios that have been proposed to account for the origin and maintenance of gay genes.

Kin selection

The mDNA theory is one of a number of theories that draw on the general notion of kin selection (Wilson, 1975; 1978). The argument is that homosexual individuals may somehow have increased the chances of successful reproduction in their relatives within ancestral environments. For example, they may have helped their siblings with resource provision and childcare, thus increasing the chances of survival of their nephews and nieces (who carry 25 per cent of their own genes). The concept of inclusive fitness refers to the fact that because we share genes with our close relatives we have a vested genetic interest in helping them. Once thought to be anti-Darwinian, altruism can also be tracked to gene survival. Genes for homosexuality may thus survive indirectly, through sibling lineages. Gay genes should therefore diminish in modern environments in which homosexuals are alienated from their families and migrate to large cities.

Although fashionable, this version of the kin selection theory is not well supported by the available evidence. Although homosexuals do seem to accrue resources and wealth (at least in the modern Western world), they do not preferentially lavish these upon relatives. Moreover, any such advantage in having homosexual family members would have to be extremely strong for the genes to survive, and they would need to demonstrate high penetrance (which they do not). Since only a quarter of our genes are shared with nephews and nieces, whereas half are shared with a son or daughter, it would take a couple of nephews or nieces to offset not producing one child, yet there is no evidence that the siblings of gay men have more children than families with no gay members. Moreover, if certain individuals were to expend efforts on assisting siblings, it would make more sense for them to be asexual and not to waste time on the complicated and time-consuming activity of being sexually attracted to and pursuing members of the same sex.

An interesting prediction from the kin selection theory is that homo-sexuals should show evidence of greater willingness and desire to help their kin. One study showed that homosexual men were, on average, more generally empathic than heterosexuals (Salais and Fischer, 1995) but this tells us little about their desire to help their nearest kin in particular. David Bobrow and J. Michael Bailey (of Northwestern University) tested the kin selection theory more directly by asking 57 heterosexual men and 66 gay men questions about their general feelings of closeness to their family, their willingness to give financial and emotional resources to members of their family, how much help they had in turn received, and their willingness to provide things such as money, gifts and help with childcare (e.g. babysitting) to their nephews and nieces. The researchers found no evidence that gay men were preferentially generous to their relatives compared to hetero-sexual men on any measure. Thus a central prediction of the kin selection theory is unsupported.

Parental manipulation

A second set of theories focuses on parental manipulation of offspring sexual orientation, such that having homosexual children benefits parents' further reproduction (Trivers, 1974). The key premise here is that parents induce homosexuality by regulating resources or socializing offspring to make them less competitive in reproductive roles, but increase their assis-tance towards reproducing siblings. In particular, this might be supposed to happen in large families where there are more potentially 'expendable' (reproductively speaking) offspring. Unfortunately, this theory assumes a primary role for psychosocial influences in the development of homosexual-ity, which we have pretty much debunked in Chapter 2. Also, although in modern times many parents may be open-minded and tolerate homosexual children, it seems unlikely that parents would willingly encourage homo-sexuality in their own offspring. Apart from the stigma that they and their children might suffer, the help provided would have to be substantial to offset the loss of the children's own direct breeding potential.

Balanced polymorphism

The paradox remains. The stability of homosexuality suggests that it is not maladaptive, yet a simple reproductive analysis argues that it is. A solution might be found in the idea of balanced polymorphism. This can be illus-trated by way of example. In African and Asian populations there exist genes that predispose to the disease of sickle-cell anaemia. These genes do not appear to have been selected against, even though they kill many individuals before reproductive age. However, possessing one variation (an allele) of the sickle-cell gene confers resistance to malaria, which in African and Asian populations causes more fatalities before reproductive age than does sickle-cell anaemia. This mechanism is referred to as balanced superior heterozygotic fitness, whereby possessing one allele of an otherwise lethal gene is balanced against its reproductive benefits.

Jim McKnight, of the University of Western Sydney (1997), has suggested that for homosexuality to survive, the genes for it must confer benefit to heterosexual individuals. He argues that heterosexual men who possess one gay allele have an enhanced sex drive which leads to greater reproductive output and the retention of balanced homosexuality gene(s). It follows, according to McKnight, that male homosexuals would also have higher sex drives than heterosexuals and their greater turnover of partners could be construed as evidence for this. However, it seems more likely that gay men have more partners because of greater opportunity and the absence of female restraint, rather than any excess of libido (Symons, 1979; Bailey *et al.*, 1994). McKnight suggests that female mate choice is a factor in maintaining gay gene(s) where the greater charm, seductiveness and sex drive of 'homosexually enabled' males is counterbalanced by women's avoidance of feminine men. Women do claim to prefer feminine behavioural traits in their partners (e.g. empathy, considerateness and expressiveness: Sprecher *et al.*, 1994) and feminized facial features in men (Perrett *et al.*, 1998; Rhodes *et al.*, 2000), presumably because loyalty, support and willingness to share resources are important to them and the prospects of their offspring. At the same time, some women notoriously gravitate towards macho, psychopathic males, ranging from wife-beaters to serial killers, because they 'smell' the testosterone. This would support the kind of trade-off implied by McKnight. However, a problem with McKnight's account is that it relies on a genetic model of homosexuality that assumes two alleles, and this is not consonant with the current genetic evidence. Also, it says nothing about lesbians.

Another version of this theory, along the lines of balanced polymorphism, has been proposed by Edward M. Miller of the University of New Orleans (2000). Miller argues that sexual orientation is influenced by a number of genes (i.e. is polygenetic) and that during development these affect the sensitivity of the male brain to sex hormones, shifting it in a feminine direction. Possessing several such alleles produces homosexuality, whereas single alleles make for greater sensitivity, empathy and kindness. That is, having too many feminizing alleles would tip a male over the threshold into homosexuality, whereas having just a few of these alleles would keep males on the 'straight' side but with the advantages of certain feminine personality traits. These would make heterosexual carriers better fathers and more attractive mates. Thus a balanced polymorphism is maintained whereby the feminizing effect of such alleles in heterosexuals counterbalances the adverse effects of these alleles in producing homosexuality. Some fancy calculations show that all that would be needed is a 2 per cent fertility advantage over other heterosexuals to ensure that gay genes survived (Mac-Intrye and Estep, 1993). The same mechanism might apply to genes that promote traits such as competitiveness as well as lesbianism in women. In this view, the birth-order effect apparent in male homosexuality (see Chapter 6) could arise as a by-product of the mechanism which shifts personalities in the feminine direction in later-born sons, reducing inter-sibling competition. The model demands evidence of those traits that increase reproductive output in heterosexual males to be shown by gay men and, indeed, there is some evidence that gay men are more empathic, sensitive and less aggressive than heterosexual men (Gladue and Bailey, 1995; Salais and Fischer, 1995). The biological mechanism (sexual development of the brain under the action of sex hormones) which links homosexuality and feminine traits may make it difficult to gain the benefits of one without the occasional reproductive costs of the other.

Baker and Bellis (1995) have reported higher reproductive output for young (under 25 years of age) bisexual females; they suggested that genes for homosexuality 'represent the maladaptive tip of an adaptive bisexual iceberg'. Homosexual activity is assumed to provide practice for later heterosexual mating. Although this theory conflicts with the bimodal nature of male sexual orientation, the data for females are interesting, given their greater rates of bisexuality, and could account for the pattern of familiality described by Pattatucci and Hamer (1995).

The value of same-sex bonding

There remains a significant problem with the above theories: they have largely failed to discuss the ancestral conditions under which selection of genes for homosexuality is presumed to have occurred. In other words, what were the adaptive problems faced by our hominid ancestors that fostered the exploitation of genetic mutations related to sexual brain development and ultimately, along with an array of other traits, homosexuality? Recently Frank Muscarella (1999) and R.C. Kirkpatrick (2000) have proposed, broadly, that homosexual behaviour was selected for because it aided same-sex affiliation and alliance formation. This, in turn, solved adaptive problems centred around social interchange, particularly inter-group and intra-sex (especially for males) conflict. Same-sex alliances are argued to have reproductive and resource accrual advantages. For example, a disposition for homoerotic behaviour could have evolved because it increased same-sex affiliation among marginalized adolescent hominids, increased access to resources, and thus indirectly increased reproductive success. Homosexual behaviour and emotional attachment serve to reinforce these same-sex bonds.

It seems true that early hominids often engaged in aggressive and fatal inter-group and intra-sex encounters, particularly among males, and that infanticide was common. Such conflict and violence could therefore have been conducive to the development of homosexual behaviour by promoting same-sex affiliation and alliances (and hence increasing reproductive success). Evidence from primates supports this scenario, pointing to a persistent (in evolutionary time) adaptive problem that hominids could have faced. Primate homosexuality is known for its role in the reduction of intra-sex aggression and increases in same-sex bonding in both natural and laboratory settings, perhaps most conspicuously in our nearest relative, the bonobo (Vasey, 1995; Bagemihl, 1999). The difference between bonobos (genetically closest to humans) and regular chimps on the other side of the Congo is that bonobos seem to use sexual behaviour for many social purposes that are more to do with bonding and defusing aggression than reproduction as such. Most obviously, the females seem to use sex with each other to build a 'sisterhood' that forms the basis of a power structure to rival that of the males. Homosexual behaviour could therefore have developed as part of a wider bisexual repertoire in early hominids, a necessary condition since opposite-sex pairings are reproductive.

How much can we learn from animal behaviour?

There are many incorrect assumptions concerning the issue of animal homosexuality. In his book *Biological Exuberance: Animal Homosexuality and Natural Diversity* (1999), Bruce Bagemihl catalogues over 300 vertebrate species in which homosexual behaviour occurs. This seems like a large number and implies a very broad incidence of homosexuality in non-humans, which in turn might be taken as evidence for some definitive evolutionary basis. In reality, although homosexual behaviour is observed in many species, it usually occurs only occasionally, and under special circumstances, rather than regularly, so some of Bagemihl's observations may be overestimates. As we have pointed out earlier, homosexual behaviour does not necessarily imply a homosexual orientation. Animals seldom show consistent homosexual preferences in the way that gay men and lesbians do, although sheep (more specifically rams, and a few other mammalian species) seem to be a notable exception (see Chapter 7). Also, the incidence of homosexual behaviour is not consistent across different animal species. Rather, it shows all kinds of variations: the type of activity (genital rubbing in monkeys), how much it occurs, and so on. Sometimes males show more homosexual behaviour; in other species it is mostly the females. Paul Vasey from the University of Lethbridge notes that the function of homosexual behaviour also differs between species. As noted above, in bonobos homosexual behaviour advances inclusion in a social group. Female bonobos tend to move from their mother's social group to a new one at puberty where they try and seek out a dominant female for homosexual activity. This helps to reinforce social bonds and allows integration into the new group. On the other hand, homosexual behaviour in the Japanese macaque monkey appears to serve no function beyond simple erotic pleasure: it does not influence entry to or expulsion from a group, or contribute to the formation of social bonds or alliances in any way at all. Naturally, this may all depend on other aspects of the 'mating psychology' of mammals, argues Bagemihl. Exclusive lifelong homosexual pairings may be uncommon for the same reasons that exclusive heterosexual pairings are: monogamy is simply not a common mating system among mammals. Overall, we need to be very careful in using animal examples to support particular evolutionary explanations we are trying to make (however much they help to inspire or narrow down possible adaptive arguments).

Again, we are struck by the remarkable parallel with hand preferences. Although certain individual animals may favour one paw over the other to catch a fish or open a door, it is just as likely to be the left paw as the right. The consistent (genetically based) predominance of right-handedness, along with an equally consistent (and equally genetic) minority preference of left-handedness, is pretty much unique to humans, connecting as it does with lateralization of the brain for speech.

A new scenario

Returning to the central discussion of this chapter, we note that Muscarella and Kirkpatrick assume a 'basic bisexuality' in modern humans, and they reject the notion of a bimodal sexual orientation in favour of a continuous one. This is inconsistent with the evidence for the clearly bimodal pattern to male sexual orientation discussed in Chapter 1, even though the female distribution does seem more variable.

Rahman and Wilson (2003a) have proposed another account along the lines of the above. We begin with the premise that intra-sex aggression constituted the adaptive problem that needed solving because it led to reduced individual survival and infanticide. Genetic mutations arose which exploited a biological mechanism determining how the body, brain and behaviour become sexually differentiated (see Chapter 5). A genotype emerged, of ancestral males who were more feminine in behavioural traits as well as bisexual in sexual preference. These traits aided same-sex affiliation and allowed certain males to maintain alliances. Females were attracted to these males because of their feminine qualities (loyalty, kindness and reduced aggression), and with the concomitant reduced infanticide, greater parenting skills, commitment and affiliation with other powerful males, the viability of their offspring was increased.

At this point we invoke the concept of *sexually antagonistic selection*, whereby selection of optimal traits in one sex favours genes that incidentally lower fitness when expressed in the other. This means that selection cannot remove these traits (Rice, 1992) and is a mechanism that could account for bimodal sexuality. Over ancestral time, females chose increasingly feminine traits (thus more feminizing alleles) in males, one consequence of which was to raise the possibility of exclusive homosexuality in males. This strategy allowed such 'exclusively gay alleles' to invade the population over time. In other words, alleles that enhance parenting success may invade the gene pool even though they reduce the mating success of the men that carry them (Getz, 1993). The effect on parenting success and the viability of offspring, which is of central importance to females who invest heavily in parental care and carry the 'costliest' unit of reproduction – ova – offsets the deleterious effects in males and thus maintains alleles for bimodal homosexuality in balanced polymorphism.

Similarly, female sexual selection could have produced the pattern of female sexual orientation currently observed. Selection for masculinizing alleles may well have maintained intra-female alliances with powerful females (by homosexual activity), but also increased female aggression, which could be conducive to greater care and protection of the young. This is consistent with Anne Campbell's (1999) suggestion that female aggression contributed to reproductive success because the survival of offspring depends more on maternal rather than paternal investment. Females may also have occasionally wanted to increase the genetic quality of offspring by extra-pair copulation, and to do this would require greater masculine traits, such as assertiveness and sexual novelty-seeking. Women who have many sexual partners have been shown to be more masculine than the average in childhood sex-typed behaviours, as well as higher in self-reported behavioural and physical masculinity (Mikach and Bailey, 1999). Male androgen hormones are also connected with assertiveness in women. Thus masculinizing alleles could produce a preference for variety in sexual partners along with other masculine traits. Again, the effect of such alleles that produce occasional lesbianism is counterbalanced by its advantages. Nonetheless, because women in ancestral environments would have been expected to marry and not refuse sex with their husbands (as is the case in many traditional societies today) an intermediate level of masculinizing alleles may have been selected for, producing the variable pattern of sexual preference that we call bisexuality. Such a bisexual strategy would be optimal for females in ancient ancestral environments, ensuring reproductive output in most female lineages.

The models discussed above by McKnight, Miller and ourselves are all based on the notion of threshold liability. That is, a certain concentration of genes will tip an individual male over a threshold into exclusive homosexuality (around 2 to 4 per cent of the population). The rest of the distribution comprises straight men, some of whom are 'gay-enabled' with the odd few gay genes that make them feminine enough to be attractive to women. The very term gentleman implies the value assigned by many women to men who are less aggressive and psychopathic than the typical male.

As with many evolutionary theories, testing such a theory is not easy (even though it is essential for a theory to be called scientific). One way might be to examine the variation in ratings of certain traits that could theoretically be desired by women. For example, you could ask (heterosexual) women to rate gay and straight men for the desirability or sexiness of physical traits (such as certain pheromone signatures, facial features, body shape) and to rate their faces for desirable personality attributes such as nurturance, empathy, charm and seductive appeal. We might predict from threshold liability models that ratings of these traits for gay men should show very little variance (so, for example, women might consistently rate gay men as more attractive facially, have better bodies, more nurturing faces, etc.) because they would consistently have more of the traits women desire. Ratings for straight men, on the other hand, will show greater variation according to the model because some straight men will be gay-enabled and others not. Then one could examine the reproductive success (number of children sired or number of copulations) of those straight men who are rated in the same range as gay men. In fact, gay men (and lesbians) show a mixture of masculine and feminine traits. The model also would predict that the straight brothers of gay men would show a higher frequency of gay-enabled traits. In reality, such brothers are not more feminine than other heterosexual men and there is no evidence that they have more children.

However, there is other evidence in favour of some of these threshold liability or 'balanced gene' models. Jim McKnight and Jim Malcolm's study (2000) with 60 gay men and 60 straight men (mentioned in Chapter 3) also reported that gay men tend to come from bigger families. This was driven primarily by an excess of aunts and also more male cousins, so there was a maternal line fecundity effect. Turner (1995) reported similar results in gay men – an excess of aunts on the maternal side. Now these findings are difficult to interpret. They may reflect some compensatory function in these families to offset the reproductive loss of having a gay member. McKnight's findings also go against Hamer's idea that perhaps an X-linked gay gene helps women in gay men's families to reproduce more. If it was X-linked then you would expect more daughters in the maternal lines than sons, but McKnight found that although gay men have more aunts, these aunts produce more sons rather than daughters (and there were no differences between numbers of female cousins across the lines of descent). Presumably women in these families have selected mates with gay-enabled attributes (charm, emotional sensitivity, etc.) and thus increased the net number of children (gay men tend to have more male cousins: McKnight and Malcolm, 2000) besides increasing the chances of full-blown homosexuality appearing somewhere in the family line.

Clearly, the evolutionary models described above need to rest on testable predictions and more data. However gay genes have survived, we think the fact they are still around shows that they have been quite successful in reproducing themselves, and ultimately evolutionary biology is about the successful replication of genes.

CHAPTER FIVE

Hormones in the womb

We all know that the bodies of men and women are very different. We have also come to recognize that their brains also differ, and hence their personalities and preferences. Yet at conception male and female zygotes are much the same, except for one bit of genetic material, an X or a Y chromosome. So what is it that produces such striking divergence in the bodies and minds of men and women?

For some time now it has been known that the balance of sex hormones we are exposed to during early life in the womb makes our bodies male or female, as well as determining male/female brain differences. Importantly, sex hormones are involved in setting sexual orientation by shunting brain development down a heterosexual or homosexual route. Evidence for a distinctive 'gay brain' is discussed in Chapter 7; here we outline evidence for the role of sex hormones in determining our sexual orientation. First, we need to familiarize ourselves with some basic endocrinology (the scientific study of hormones and their effects on physiology and behaviour).

How hormones work

The 'prenatal androgen theory', as it is known, proposes a major role for the male sex hormones, androgens (of which testosterone is key), in producing sexual orientation (Ellis and Ames, 1987). As we have said, the foetus is pretty much sexually indifferent at the very early stages of pregnancy. However, it is already genetically male (i.e. has an X chromosome paired with a Y chromosome) or female (has two X chromosomes). During the first two trimesters (thirds) of gestation, the foetus contains the apparatus for male and female genitalia (the Wolffian duct and Mullerian duct, respectively). At the third trimester the presence of a Y chromosome in a foetus kicks off the cascade of hormonal events that produces a recognizable male. The Y chromosome comes with a gene called Testis Determining Factor (or

TDF), which begins to make testes. The testes then begin to release the male sex hormone testosterone which masculinizes the Wolffian system so as to develop into male genitals. At the same time, another hormone (Mullerian Inhibiting Hormone) destroys the Mullerian duct. By contrast, in a female foetus (with an XX chromosome profile) the Mullerian duct develops into female genitalia without any help from sex hormones. In other words, the default gender in all mammals is female. If there is no Y chromosome (or no androgens) the foetus will develop as a female. Thus an absence of androgens results in feminization of the foetal brain.

Among the many genes that determine male sexual development, some produce the Androgen Receptor (AR) protein, which occurs in most tissues, particularly the brain. ARs mediate the actions of other sex hormones. They work like gates into other cells, allowing testosterone to enter or bind to them. This testosterone–AR 'complex' then influences the activity of other genes within the cell, determining the way the brain and body develop. Importantly, in the body and the brain testosterone may also be converted to two other powerful sex hormones. The first is dihydrotestosterone (DHT), through an enzyme (which is a biological catalyst) called 5-alpha-reductase. This is called the 5-alpha-reductase pathway. The second hormone to which testosterone can convert is oestrogen, through another enzyme called aromatase. This 'aromatized testosterone' binds to oestrogen receptors (ERs – from the US spelling 'estrogen') and acts to masculinize (increase male-like behaviours) and defeminize (reduce female-like responses) the behavioural development of male mammals. Many of these androgen and oestrogen receptors are found in the human brain but differ in their distribution and concentration between the sexes. For example, one important brain region implicated in sexual preference and sexual behaviour – the hypothalamus – has many more ARs in men than in women (Fernandez-Guasti et al., 2000).

In its simplest form, prenatal androgen theory supposes that homosexuality in males is owing to under-masculinization (the partial absence of androgenizing effects) and lesbianism in women is because of over-masculinization (excess androgenizing effects) during early brain development (Ellis and Ames, 1987). It is a common presumption that gay men are exposed to less testosterone, and lesbians to more, and these different levels influence the structure and function of brain regions that control the direction of sexual attraction. For example, homosexuality could result from fewer

ARs in the brains of gay men, meaning that testosterone cannot masculin-ize certain parts of the brain with few of these receptors. Alternatively, there might not be enough aromatase to convert testosterone to oestrogen within the male brain. One or both of these might be true, but matters are compli-cated in that certain traits (associated with male homosexuality in particular) appear 'hyper-masculine' rather than feminized. We shall dis-cuss these traits later; in the meantime, suffice it to note that while at first blush they seem counter-intuitive to the basic idea of prenatal hormone theory, there is a way to understand the apparent contradiction. If homo-sexuality occurs as a result of some failure of testosterone to penetrate one or other of the two brain systems mentioned above (the 5-alpha-reductase or aromatase pathways) then what might be observed would be heightened male traits resulting from a residue of testosterone in other brain areas, and perhaps peripheral (body) manifestations, such as hairy chests and male-pattern baldness.

How do we know that these prenatal (before birth, in the womb) sex hormones are involved in sexual orientation? There are two types of effects of sex hormones on brain and behaviour: organizational effects, which mould brain and behaviour early in the womb and are irreversible (these are the ones which determine sexual orientation), and activational effects, which are transient effects of hormones circulating in the blood upon brain and behaviour in adulthood (e.g. the well-known mood fluctuations at differ-ent stages of a woman's menstrual cycle). Homosexual and heterosexual adults cannot be reliably distinguished as regards circulating hormone levels. The prominent sex researcher Heino Meyer-Bahlburg reviewed many differ-ent studies and concluded that there were no major differences, certainly for gay men (Meyer-Bahlburg, 1984). One study by a Northumbrian group of researchers (Neave *et al.*, 1999) actually found *higher* testosterone levels in gay men compared to straight men, but this was in the context of perform-ance on certain types of mental tests (which we come to in Chapter 7) and it is unclear how they relate to basal levels. Likewise, some studies have shown higher levels of testosterone (measured by saliva samples) in lesbians com-pared with heterosexual women, and in self-described 'butch' compared with 'femme' lesbians (Singh *et al.*, 1999), yet others find no such differ-ences (Dancey, 1990). It is hard to interpret many of these studies because they take no account of the stage of the menstrual cycle that the women

71

were at. The precise relationship between prenatal levels of sex hormones and circulating levels later in adulthood is also unclear, so for the time being we cannot draw strong conclusions from these studies.

If there are no reliable differences between heterosexuals and homosexuals in the levels of sex hormones in adults, what leads to us to believe there are differences earlier in foetal life? Some research in animals gives us the first hints. These studies are generally consistent with the above findings – changing hormone levels in mammals during their adulthood has little effect on the direction of sexual preference, although they do affect sexual drive and sexual performance, such as mounting or ejaculation. However, in a now-classic study in 1959, researchers injected testosterone into female guinea pigs while they were still foetuses and found that they had masculinized genitalia, similar to normal males. When these guinea pigs became sexually mature they were injected with testosterone again. Those that had been prenatally androgenized showed substantially less female-typical sexual behaviour (particularly a behaviour called lordosis, which involves raising the rump in order to allow a male to mount her). Instead, they mounted other females (Phoenix *et al.*, 1959). So exposure to testosterone during certain sensitive 'windows' of development seems to affect the brain structures that control sexual behaviour. This type of organizing effect of sex hormones also appears in other mammals, such as rats and monkeys, although the critical periods differ between species (Goy *et al.*, 1988). Obviously, only studies in humans can definitively tell us about the role of prenatal sex hormones in human sexual orientation.

Middle-sex

Mike Bailey in his book *The Man Who Would Be Queen* has suggested a useful 'thought experiment' as the perfect test of the prenatal androgen theory. We would take a random sample of newborn males from their birth mothers; change their sex by castrating them and giving them female genitalia by surgical means. They would then be placed with adoptive parents who were not aware of the child's birth sex and reared as girls. We would then look at them in adulthood and if they were sexually attracted to women then this would be evidence that sexual orientation is hard-wired in the brain, most probably by prenatal sex hormones. A similar version of this experiment would apply to newborn girls. Obviously, this experiment could never be done in real life because it is unethical, but a mixture of medical accidents and nature has provided us with some interesting approximations.

Occasionally we have cases where baby boys have been reassigned to the female sex because they suffered an early accident to their penis (e.g. during circumcision) such that it needed to be removed. The testicles are also removed (castration) but, up until that time, have secreted their testosterone normally (which we now know is sufficient to masculinize the brains of these unfortunate individuals). The reason why these boys were (and may still be today) so readily reassigned to the gender opposite to that of their chromosomes was the prevailing medical view that with suitable upbringing and gender socialization anyone can become a boy or a girl. A famous sexologist, Dr John Money from the Johns Hopkins University Medical School (Money and Ehrhardt, 1972), was at the forefront of those who argued that sex identity was malleable, but additional justification came from the fact that surgeons found it difficult to reconstruct normal-looking penises.

Money applied his ideas in a now classic case of a boy who had his penis effectively obliterated by a botched circumcision involving electric cauterization at seven months of age. When he reached 17 months it was decided to raise the boy as a girl, and full castration and surgery to make a vagina took place at 21 months (Money and Ehrhardt, 1972; Money, 1975). Money's own follow-up concluded that the boy had more or less successfully adjusted to a female gender identity at nine years of age, and the case became celebrated as proof of the social learning origins of gender identity. However, by puberty the patient had rejected the female identity and began to live as male, and by 25 he reported full heterosexual attraction to women, and married one (Diamond, 1982; Diamond and Sigmundson, 1997). In another case, a boy had sustained extensive damage to his penis at two months caused by an accident during circumcision (Bradley et al., 1998). This was followed by castration and full genital surgery at age seven months. The study reported that the subject maintained a female gender identity at age 26 but was partially sexually attracted to women (i.e. claimed to be bisexual, but had more sexual fantasies about women: Bradley et al., 1998).

In the medical condition called cloacal exstrophy abnormalities occur in the entire pelvis region resulting in a very small penis (although intact and with normally functioning testicles). In one case study, a boy with this condition was reassigned as a girl and had apparently maintained a female gender identity and sexual attraction to males at age 17 (Vates *et al.*, 1999). However, a study with 16 genetic boys with cloacal exstrophy (of varying ages from five to 16 years), 14 of whom were reassigned as girls (13 at two weeks of age, and one by 12 weeks of age; two were not reassigned because their parents would not allow it and so they remained male), showed that ten of them declared themselves as males (8 declared fully, and two out of three were less decisive about their sexual identity). Most strikingly, all of the adolescents in this sample examined reported that they were attracted to females (Reiner and Gearhart, 2004).

These approximations to the thought experiment are, of course, limited because the child is not adopted by different parents, and the medical procedures for changing sex are not always perfect. Nonetheless, they constitute strong evidence in favour of the prenatal androgen theory that male-typical levels of sex hormones during early life in the womb produce sexual attraction towards females.

We also have 'experiments of nature' which provide further evidence in favour of the prenatal androgen theory of sexual orientation. This time, instead of looking at otherwise hormonally normal boys who have had their sex reassigned, we can look at groups of individuals who have been exposed to 'contrary' sex hormones during early development in the womb because of a specific disorder, or because of injections of extra hormones that were believed to be beneficial for at-risk pregnancies.

The condition called congenital adrenal hyperplasia (CAH) provides a most interesting case because it allows us to examine the role of prenatal sex hormones on sexual preferences while holding gender socialization reasonably constant. CAH is a genetic disorder that causes synthesis of the stress hormone cortisol in the adrenal glands to be disrupted; instead the adrenal glands release male sex hormones (particularly a hormone called androstenedione, which is converted first to testosterone and then to the powerful dihydrotestosterone). In otherwise genetic females (with an XX chromosome pattern) these excessive levels of hormones cause masculinization of the genitalia (which can range from clitoral enlargement to a fully formed penis and empty scrotum) and behaviour. In most cases, when the condition is diagnosed early, corrective surgery and hormone treatment are given and the child is raised as a normal girl. There have been many studies on the sexual orientation of CAH women, and most show elevated rates of homosexual (lesbian) preferences. John Money and colleagues (1984) found that, of 30 CAH females who were willing to disclose their sexual preferences, 48 per cent reported homosexual imagery and 22 per cent reported homosexual behaviour, compared to 7 per cent and 4 per cent respectively in control subjects. In 1992 a group of German researchers (Dittman *et al.*, 1992) gave 34 CAH females a sexual behaviour interview (covering topics like sexual fantasy, behaviour and relationships) and compared their responses to 14 normal sisters (ages ranged from 11 to 41 years old). In the whole sample, 22 per cent of the CAH females expressed an interest in having a lesbian relationship, or had had such relationships (compared with none of the sisters). In CAH females over 21 years old, 44 per cent expressed this homosexual interest. The differences could not be attributed to medical problems associated with having a poorly formed vagina, or a sense of inadequacy in heterosexual relationships. A group of Canadian researchers replicated these findings in 31 CAH women (aged 18 or over, compared with 15 unaffected sisters or female cousins). They reported significantly higher rates of homosexual fantasy, less sexual experience with men but no differences in reported sexual experiences with women compared to controls (Zucker *et al.*, 1996). Overall, these data suggest that excessive exposure to prenatal male sex hormones does cause shifts in sexual orientation in a male-typical direction. Nonetheless, in these studies sexual orientation is not entirely homosexual. Given the large amounts of prenatal androgens these women had been exposed to (often in the male-typical range) it is surprising that larger shifts in sexual orientation were not reported. Zucker and colleagues wondered if there might have been some under-reporting of the homosexual preference because it is less socially acceptable.

One way of controlling for the effects of ambiguous genitalia (and thus, the idea of a different gender socialization based on genital appearance) is to examine women whose mothers had taken the drug diethylstilbestrol (or DES). DES was widely used treat at-risk pregnancies during the mid twentieth century until its use was stopped in 1971 because of its severe side-effects, including cancer. Although a synthetic oestrogen, DES is a masculinizing agent in women, bypassing the known mechanisms which protect female foetuses from masculinizing hormones. However, being less strong than the androgens causing CAH, it does not produce male-like genitalia. Studies have consistently shown elevated rates of bisexual or homosexual attraction and fantasy in DES women compared to controls, although many of these women did not self-identify as bisexual or lesbian and the responses were more bisexual rather than exclusively homosexual (Ehrhardt *et al.*, 1985; Meyer-Bahlburg *et al.*, 1995).

Another intersexual condition, which represents a rather extreme form of feminization in genetic males, is androgen insensitivity syndrome (or AIS). In the 'complete' version of this disorder (CAIS) genetic males are completely insensitive to the effects of prenatal androgens because of a genetic defect in the androgen receptor gene. These individuals turn out convincingly female in almost every way: they have female genitalia (except for an absence of pubic hair), female body features and female-like behaviour. However, they are infertile (having XY chromosomes) and have undescended testes, which are usually removed surgically, since they are nearly always raised as girls. Several studies show that in adulthood almost all CAIS women report sexual attraction to men. A study in the US with 14 CAIS women reported that all bar one reported heterosexual attraction, fantasy and behaviour (Wisniewski *et al.*, 2000). In a study conducted in the UK with a large sample, Melissa Hines of City University, London, and her colleagues at the University of Cambridge recruited 22 women with CAIS and compared them to 22 controls matched for age, race and sex of rearing. The researchers reported that CAIS women had heterosexual erotic interests and were as likely to be married or living with a male partner as the female controls (Hines *et al.*, 2003). There were no differences between CAIS women and controls in psychological well-being, suggesting that psychological factors play no role in their sexual orientation. The CAIS data are powerful evidence supporting the prenatal androgen theory because they show that a lack of androgen action leads to sexual attraction towards men. However, it is not a perfect test of the thought experiment as CAIS females are also reared as girls.

Overall, these studies of intersexual conditions support the idea that too much androgen in genetic females (CAH) and too little or none in genetic males (CAIS) produce elevated rates of homosexuality. Other factors, such as ambiguous genitalia or psychological well-being, are unlikely to account for the differences between patient samples and controls.

Finger lengths

Further evidence that prenatal sex hormones are involved in human sexual orientation comes from an unlikely source – the length of your fingers. In particular, the relative length of the index finger to the ring finger (the ratio of second to fourth finger lengths, or 2D:4D ratio) seems to be important. This ratio is sexually dimorphic, being lower in men than women. That is, men typically have a stubbier index finger relative to their ring finger, whereas in females these fingers tend to be more or less the same length (see Figure 5.1). The fingers are usually measured from the lowest crease above the palm to the tip of the finger (not including the nails), and the ratio is calculated by dividing the length of the forefinger by that of the ring finger (2D/4D).

Figure 5.1. The left image shows the female-typical finger-length ratio (2D:4D) pattern and the right image the male-typical finger-length ratio pattern.

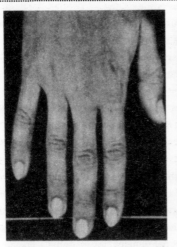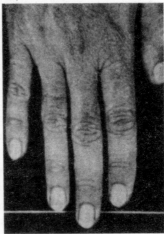

This male–female difference is well established by the age of two, and probably before birth (perhaps as early the 14th week of gestation: Manning *et al.*, 1998, Manning *et al.*, 2000; Manning, 2002). It seems to be determined by the balance of sex hormones *in utero* – more androgens promoting a male-like 2D:4D and more oestrogen causing a female-like 2D:4D. At its origin are genes (the Homeobox genes Hox a and Hox d) common to both the differentiation of the urinary-genital system (which therefore may influence early production of testicular androgens) and the formation of digits.

In a pioneering study of the psychological implications of the finger-length ratio, Wilson (1983) reasoned that if body and brain were jointly influenced by prenatal sex hormones, then within-sex variation in the finger-length ratio might predict gendered personality traits. This hypothesis was confirmed by the finding that women with atypical (male-like) finger ratios were more assertive and competitive (masculine traits) than other women. More recently, CAH women (who have been exposed to excessive androgens) have been shown to have male-like ratios (Brown *et al.*, 2002). One study by John Manning from the University of Central Lancashire (currently a leading expert on finger-length ratios) and his colleagues from the University of Cambridge examined foetal testosterone and foetal oestrogen levels from the amniotic fluid of pregnant mothers. They then measured the finger lengths of their children at two years of age. They found that a low 2D:4D was related to higher levels of foetal testosterone relative to oestrogen levels, and vice versa for high 2D:4D (Lutchmaya *et al.*, 2004). Manning also reports that low 2D:4D is linked to sensitivity to testosterone, as indicated by variation in the genetic structure of the androgen receptor gene (Manning *et al.*, 2003). All in all, there is strong evidence that finger-length ratios are indicative of prenatal sex hormone levels and they are of special interest because there is no way they could be affected by learning or psychological factors. 2D:4D ratios are linked to several sex-dependent disorders, including medical conditions such as heart disease, breast cancer and autism (see Manning, 2002, for a full review).

How, then, do finger ratios relate to sexual orientation? The most straightforward prediction would be that gay men would show a low-androgen, 'feminine' pattern compared with straight men, and that lesbians would approximate to the male-typical pattern. Unfortunately, the facts are not that simple. Terrance Williams and colleagues from the University of California at Berkeley sampled 720 male and female volunteers at a public street fair in San Francisco, asking them about their sexual orientation, age, handedness, and the number and sex of children their mothers had carried before them (Williams *et al.*, 2000). Finger lengths were measured from photocopies of their hands by researchers who were unaware of the volunteers' sexual orientations. The expected sex difference in the 2D:4D ratio was observed in a comparison of 108 straight men with 146 straight women, although it was greater on the right hand than the left. (Perhaps, as the primary human manipulator, the right hand, in right-handed persons, is more sensitive to prenatal androgens.) Williams *et al.* (2000) also found that the right-hand 2D:4D ratio in 164 lesbians was significantly lower (i.e. more 'masculine') than that of 146 heterosexual women, and no different from that of heterosexual men. Overall, homosexual and heterosexual men were not distinguished, but segregating them by birth order revealed that later-born gay men with two or more older brothers had a more masculine right-hand finger ratio than gay men with one or no older brothers. On the basis of this birth-order effect, the authors concluded that men with older brothers, including those who may become gay, are exposed to higher prenatal testosterone levels. There were no associations between finger lengths ratios and handedness or age.

Subsequent studies have produced somewhat confusing results. Robinson and Manning (2000) and the present authors (Rahman and Wilson, 2003b) found *masculinized* 2D:4D ratios in gay men compared to heterosexuals, and these were unrelated to birth order. In our sample of 240 healthy Londoners, we also found that lesbians showed masculinized 2D:4D ratios, as did another study by Dennis McFadden and Erin Schubel (2002) of the University of Texas at Austin. By contrast, McFadden and Schubel found *feminized* 2D:4D ratios for gay men. In a very large study of over 2,000 volunteers (heterosexuals recruited from university sources and gay/lesbian volunteers from gay pride festivals), Richard Lippa of California State University also found feminized 2D:4D ratios in gay men compared to heterosexual men and no differences between lesbians and heterosexual women (Lippa, 2003).

Overall, it seems that lesbians do have greater exposure to prenatal androgens than heterosexual women (three to one of the studies in favour of this). But what are we to make of the data for gay men – some showing 'hyper-male' 2D:4D, and others female-like patterns? A partial reconciliation may come from the cross-ethnic comparisons of Manning and Robinson (2003), which show considerably greater race differences in the 2D:4D ratio for heterosexual than gay men. Gay men showed a fairly standard mean 2D:4D ratio of 0.96–0.97; hence this narrow range (slightly on the masculine side) seems to be associated with the prenatal hormonal mix that maximizes the chances of homosexuality. The work McFadden and Schubel hinted that finger-length ratios other than 2D:4D might also be important (e.g. 2D:5D and 3D:4D).

While it makes intuitive sense that higher prenatal androgens would predispose to lesbianism in women, the observation that homosexuality in men is sometimes associated with high androgen levels is rather surprising. Surely gay men should be exposed to *less* prenatal androgens? The paradox might be resolved, however, if it is supposed that barriers against androgens with respect to the masculinization of certain brain structures (notably those concerned with sexual orientation) lead to increased secretion in an effort to break through, or some of kind of accumulation elsewhere. That is, if brain structures responsible for direction of sexual preference (as well as other behavioural traits) are left unmasculinized, either because of reduced sensitivity to androgens or lack of conversion to masculinizing oestrogens, then there may be excess testosterone left in other departments. This might explain certain 'hyper-male' body features that have been observed (albeit unreliably) in gay men, including masculinized finger-length ratios, hair distribution and genital size. A pathway whereby testosterone is converted to dihydrotestosterone (DHT) is very likely involved in these processes. We will see later that Dennis McFadden of the University of Texas at Austin makes a similar point regarding the apparent masculinization of some aspects of gay men's auditory systems. The point to bear in mind is that homosexuality appears as a mosaic of traits (some sex-*typical*, others sex-*atypical* and yet others that are sex-*exaggerated*), all produced by apparently contradictory effects of prenatal sex hormones. Certainly, it is simplistic to think of gay men are just like straight women, and lesbians as like straight men, in brain and body differentiation.

Fingerprints

Another window into early prenatal development is the pattern of skin ridges found on the palms and soles of all primates, including humans. The study of skin ridges is known as dermatoglyphics. Dermatoglyphic characteristics develop between the eighth and 16th weeks of gestation, so if we should discover consistent differences between homosexuals and heterosexuals, this might provide clues as to the developmental phase at which sexual orientation is laid down. Mostly, it is fingerprints that are used, and these are measured by pressing the fingers and thumb on an inkpad and printing them on a standard form like that used by the police. The number of ridges is counted on both hands using a magnifying glass and a standard system of quantifying ridge counts called the Henry classification (see Figure 5.2).

....

Figure 5.2. Fingerprint ridge count is often measured from the triradius (point at which ridges form together in a triangular formation) to the centre of the fingerprint pattern; one counts each ridge which crosses the line.

....

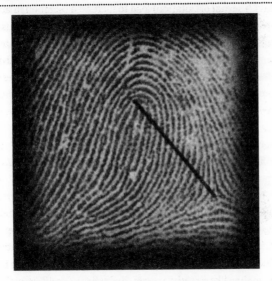

For dermatoglyphics to connect with sexual orientation via the prenatal androgen theory they would have to be related to prenatal sex hormone levels. Unfortunately, it is not clear that they are. Men typically have higher ridge counts than women on both hands, yet monkeys injected prenatally with testosterone show lower ridge counts (Jamison *et al.*, 1994). Dermatoglyphic patterns are also affected by other factors, especially genetics, but also maternal stress, drug and alcohol use (Forastieri *et al.*, 2003). Thus dermatoglyphic traits might be indicators of the general state of early biological development, rather than effects of prenatal sex hormones specifically.

Although men typically have more ridges than women, the dermato-glyphic profiles of heterosexuals and homosexuals are not consistently differentiated. An initial study by J.A.Y. Hall and Doreen Kimura (1994) of the University of Western Ontario, Canada, found greater leftward asymmetry (more ridges on the left fingers) in gay men than heterosexual men, a pattern often found in women. Leftward asymmetry was also associated with non-right-handedness in gay men but not in heterosexual men. These data were taken as suggestive of an atypical intrauterine environment being experienced by homosexuals. Subsequent studies in the US and Europe, using larger samples and stricter procedures, have failed to replicate Hall and Kimura's early findings (Slabbekoorn *et al.*, 2000; Mustanski *et al.*, 2002 Forastieri *et al.*, 2003), while others have reported contrary results (Green and Young, 2000). All these studies (including Hall and Kimura's) found no sexual-orientation-related differences in total ridge count – the dermatoglyphic feature by which the sexes differ most clearly. Thus finger-print patterns do not seem to afford us a reliable window on early prenatal differentiation of sexual orientation in humans.

Auditory mechanisms

Further evidence for the role of prenatal sex hormones in sexual orientation is provided by an auditory phenomenon called otoacoustic emissions (or OAEs). OAEs are weak sounds emitted by the inner ear, which can either occur spontaneously or be elicited by a 'click' stimulus. These sounds are so weak that you are usually unaware of them; they can only be detected by a sensitive microphone placed inside the ear canal (see Figure 5.3). OAEs, both the spontaneous and click-evoked, are typically more numerous in females than in males and in the right ear than the left. These sex and ear differences exist in infants, children and adults, and hence are stable throughout life (McFadden and Pasanen, 1998; 1999). Evidence that OAEs are related to prenatal sex hormones comes from studies showing that females who had male co-twins (who are thus exposed to more androgens in the womb) have masculinized OAE patterns. This implicates prenatal androgens for masculinizing the inner ear (most notably the cochleae: McFadden, 1993).

Dennis McFadden and Edward Pasenen of the University of Texas at Austin are leaders in this field. In their first study, examining click-evoked OAEs (or CEOAEs) McFadden and Pasenen tested 237 heterosexual and homosexual men and women, assessing sexual orientation with the Kinsey scales. Hearing was checked for normality and volunteers were asked not to take any drugs or expose themselves to loud sounds for 24 hours before testing. They were then exposed to several clicks and a microphone recorded their CEOAE responses, which were filtered and analysed by computer. No differences were found in the CEOAEs of gay and heterosexual men, but the CEOAEs of lesbians (and in this study bisexual women) were less numerous and weaker than those of heterosexual women (McFadden and Pasanen, 1998). In other words, the CEOAEs of lesbian women were masculinized. Another study using the same sample, McFadden and Pasanen (1999), confirmed that the spontaneous OAEs (SOAEs) in lesbian and bisexual women were masculinized compared to heterosexual women. Again there were no differences in the SOAEs of gay and straight men.

Figure 5.3. Recording OAEs from a volunteer (Photography courtesy of Dennis McFadden, University of Texas at Austin).

A further study by the Texas group examined another auditory phenomenon known as auditory evoked potentials (AEPs). These are electrical brain responses to click stimuli recorded from electrodes placed on the scalp. Changes in electrical potentials in response to the sound result in a series of peaks or waves, which can be visualized on computer, and which represent different groups of neurons firing more or less in synchrony. McFadden and Champlin (2000) recorded AEPs from 49 heterosexual women, 57 lesbian and bisexual women, 50 heterosexual men and 53 gay (and bisexual) men and produced 19 AEP measures. For five of the 19 measures the responses of lesbian/bisexual women were male-typical compared to heterosexual women. For gay men, five out of the 19 measures were hyper-masculinized compared to heterosexual men.

So it looks as though the brains (at least those regions controlling auditory processing) and cochleae of lesbian women (or we should say non-heterosexual women, as bisexuals were included here) are masculinized. For gay men the picture is different – the OAEs of gay men are sex-typical, just like those of straight men, but the part of the brain that regulates auditory processing seems to be more masculinized. Again we find a 'hyper-male' pattern in gay men. In line with our suggestion above concerning finger-length ratios, Dennis McFadden (2002) argues that the feminization of sexual preference in gay men is associated with too much, not too little, androgen in some areas. This means that gay men might show a number of differences in various markers that are in female-typical directions (such as certain measures of growth, which we shall explore next), but others that are in the hyper-male direction. These are called non-monotonic effects. In gerbils the type of paw stance the animal takes differs between the sexes –males rest more on their right forepaw and females more on the left forepaw. Injecting male gerbils with testosterone early in life produces the female-typical pattern of paw preference, so being exposed to excess androgens pushes the male animal towards sex-atypical behaviour (Clark *et al.*, 1996). Such mosaic patterns of traits in homosexuals could occur because the features are affected differently by localized differences in concentration of androgens or different localized sensitivity of the sex hormone receptors at certain 'critical' times during foetal development and not others.

Do gay men have bigger penises?

If gay men are exposed to more prenatal androgens than heterosexual men, could there be differences in the size of the genitalia between these two groups of men? The answer appears to be yes, which is perhaps good news for one group and not the other! We already know that excessive exposure to prenatal androgens in CAH women produces differences in genital size and shape in the male-typical direction. In a study conducted in the 1960s Nedoma and Freund (1961) examined the penis sizes of 126 gay men and 86 heterosexual men. Measurements were made by a physician, and gay men were found to have significantly larger penises than heterosexual men. In 1999 the sex researchers Anthony Bogaert of Brock University in Canada and Scott Herschberger of California State University published a paper on penis size using the extensive Kinsey archives, which contain data on a number of psychological and physical traits in over 5,000 heterosexual and homosexual research volunteers from the 1940s and 1950s. They compared 935 gay men and 4,187 heterosexual men on five self-reported measures of erect and flaccid penis length and circumference. The male volunteers did the measurements on themselves using measuring rulers or tape. Bogaert and Hershberger found that on all measures gay men reported larger penises than heterosexual men. For example, gay men reported an estimated erect penis length of 6.32 inches (standard deviation of 0.95) compared to 5.99 inches (standard deviation of 0.91) for heterosexual men. Bogaert and Herschberger's results held up after controlling for age, education, height and weight differences between the two groups of men.

Could these results could be due self-reporting biases, gay men overestimating their penis sizes because they are more concerned with the male organ or to conform to an ideal standard of sexual attractiveness? Although gay men may be more concerned about certain aspects of their physiques, heterosexual men are also concerned about the size of their penises, and there is no reason to assume that self-reporting biases account for the differences. The results of Bogaert and Hershberger replicate those of the independent study by Nedoma and Freund in which penis size was measured objectively. Again, this apparent hyper-masculinization of penis size in gay men could be explained by the paradoxical effects of male sex hormones discussed by McFadden (2002). It is also compatible with a version of the prenatal androgen theory of sexual orientation we outlined earlier. Male rhesus monkeys that are exposed to higher levels of androgens later in prenatal development (but not at earlier stages) also tend to have larger penis size, confirming a role for prenatal androgens in penile growth (Herman *et al.*, 2000). It is likely that other hormones (such as growth hormones secreted from the thyroid gland) and genetic factors play some role also.

Physical growth

Further evidence for a role for sex hormones in sexual orientation is provided by data on weight and height differences between heterosexuals and
homosexuals. Weight and height are sexually dimorphic variables, with
men being taller and heavier than women on average. Some of the brain
structures responsible for behaviour that differs between the sexes also
controls aspects of growth via a brain 'circuit' called the hypothalamic-
pituitary-gonadal axis. Hence the growth of bone mass, musculature and
weight distribution (including the regulation of fat content) may be different in homosexuals compared to heterosexuals. Several studies show that
gay men are, on average, lighter and shorter than heterosexual men (Blanchard and Bogaert, 1996b; Bogaert and Blanchard, 1996) while lesbians
are, on average, heavier and taller than heterosexual women (Bogaert,
1998a). These studies have typically used large samples, or looked at data
from the extensive Kinsey archives, but they have relied primarily on self-
reported measurements or estimates of weight and height. Also, the
differences are relatively small. For gay versus straight men the weight
difference is about five kilograms, while the height difference is about 1.5
centimetres (adjusted for mothers' and fathers' height: Bogaert and Blanchard, 1996). For lesbians versus straight women the weight difference is
about two kilograms and the height difference is less than one centimetre
(Bogaert, 1998). Another study used data from the British National Survey
of Sexual Attitudes and Lifestyles (Natsal), comprising a very large national
probability sample, broadly representative of the British population
(Bogaert and Friesen, 2002). No differences were found in height and
weight between gay and heterosexual men, while lesbians differed only in
being taller (approximately one centimetre) than heterosexual women.

The findings on height and weight differences are therefore mixed, and
at least for weight it is unclear whether any possible sexual-orientation-
related differences are down to the effects of sex hormones or an effect of
psychological factors. Gay men are typically very concerned about their
physiques and tend to have a higher rate of eating disorders; hence a pre-
occupation with thinness and dieting might cause lower weight in gay men.

Although the height differences appear no more robust than the weight
differences, final adult height is less likely to be influenced by environmental
and psychological factors, so perhaps sexual-orientation-related differences

here are more reflective of genetic or other organizational factors. One recent study has rather definitively answered some of these questions regarding height and weight differences. James Martin and Duc Huu Nguyen of the Western University of Health Sciences in California recruited exclusively heterosexual (118 men and 109 women) and exclusively homosexual (117 gay men and 68 lesbians) subjects from several sites in Washington, DC, Southern California and West Virginia (Martin and Nguyen, 2004). The researchers looked at several anthropometric markers (according to standard criteria and using instruments such as callipers) including pelvic width, arm length, hand width and length, overall height, weight and body mass index (BMI) as an estimate of bone size. The relative size of bones in adulthood reflects the levels of sex hormone and growth hormone actions during early childhood, if not earlier. For example, testosterone augments the stimulation of growth-related factors in boys. Thus these bone-related markers may be useful in identifying variations in early sex hormone exposure. The study found no differences in height between heterosexuals and homosexuals, although the authors reported a trend (statistically non-significant) for heterosexual men and lesbians to be taller than gay men and heterosexual women. However, heterosexual men and lesbians were significantly heavier, with higher BMIs than gay men and heterosexual women. In terms of bone growth, gay men and heterosexual women had less bone growth in the arms, legs and hands compared to heterosexual men and lesbians. Although males had greater trunk growth (waist to neck line) and wider shoulders than women overall, there were no sexual orientation differences. Pelvic width did not relate to sexual orientation.

These differences almost certainly reflect differences in the actions of sex hormones early during the development of sexual dimorphism in skeletal size and shape. Oestrogen and androgen receptors are widely present in bones, and early androgen treatment in female rats increases body weight and tibial length, whereas the converse occurs in male rats that are castrated early in life. Martin and Nguyen argue that sexual dimorphism of long bone growth of the arms and legs emerges before puberty (at around eight years of age) whereas differences in measures such as trunk size emerge primarily during puberty where there are massive rises in the levels of sex hormones. Thus the heterosexual–homosexual differences in bone growth in the arms and legs (but not in trunk size or shoulder width) probably reflect different levels of hormonal signals during childhood.

The pattern of these traits is clearly different from those for finger-length ratios for men. Gay men appear partially feminized in weight and bone growth. Lesbians, as usual, appear masculinized in these traits. As discussed above, these mosaic-like effects probably arise from varying levels of sex hormone exposure and varying critical windows for the development of the respective traits.

Onset of puberty

Another growth-related measure on which differences appear between heterosexuals and homosexuals (at least for men) is the timing of the arrival of puberty. Pubertal onset is sexually dimorphic, with boys typically reaching puberty later than girls. If the brain structures responsible for pubertal timing are feminized in men and masculinized in women, then we might expect earlier pubertal onset in gay men (compared with heterosexual men) and later pubertal onset in lesbians (compared with heterosexual women). Studies in this area again rely on self-reports, but the findings for men are mostly consistent. With men, researchers ask participants to state at what age the following occurred: first ejaculation, first pubic hair growth and voice breaking. Gay men report earlier pubertal onset on most of these indices compared to heterosexual men, both in large contemporary samples (including national probability studies) and the Kinsey archives (Blanchard and Bogaert, 1996b; Bogaert and Blanchard, 1996; Bogaert et al., 2002). Another behavioural indicator, age of first sexual experience, also suggests earlier puberty in gay men (Bogaert and Friesen, 2002). The differences between gay and straight men are small, about 2.5 months on average. For women, researchers mostly asked when they had their first menstruation, but other measures such as first pubic hair growth and first sexual experience were sometimes also taken. On none of these milestones of puberty do lesbians differ from heterosexual women (Bogaert, 1998a; Tenhula and Bailey, 1998; Bogaert et al., 2002; Bogaert and Freisen, 2002).

Apparently, then, gay men are slightly 'feminized' with respect to pubertal onset. This could arise from early prenatal feminization of the brain circuitry (especially the hypothalamic-pituitary-gonadal axis) setting the timing for pubertal onset in gay men earlier than for straight men. However, this explanation is problematic. It is thought that, in males, puberty is marked by an increase in a hormone releasing factor called gonadotropin-releasing hormone (GnRH) from the front portion of the brain structure called the hypothalamus. This factor stimulates the release of testosterone from the testes, which completes the adult sexual development of boys. But if gay men have a more female-like hypothalamus (explored in more detail in Chapter 7) this would mean they would have less GnRH release and thus less testosterone secretion. In effect, gay men should show delayed rather than earlier pubertal onset. However, if gay men are exposed to more pre-natal testosterone (as indicated by finger-length ratios) then perhaps certain parts of the brain that are responsible for male pubertal onset are hyper-masculinized, thus producing the precocious onset found in gay men. So perhaps, for men, early pubertal onset is a hyper-male trait rather than a feminized one.

All in all, pubertal timing is very complex and still poorly understood. Nonetheless, something seems to be going on prenatally to produce the differences in onset between gay and straight men. The pubertal differences between the two groups of men may relate to the differences in bone growth in the legs. As boys typically have a longer period of growth before puberty, this could allow more time for leg growth. The observation that hetero-sexual men have longer leg-bone growth could be a result of the additional couple of months before they enter puberty relative to gay men.

Maternal stress and substance use

One longstanding theory about homosexuality proposes that the amount of stress a mother experiences during pregnancy will affect the chances of her unborn child becoming gay or lesbian. It is argued that this prenatal stress affects the foetal hormonal environment and alters the balance of sex hormones in such a way that the chances of homosexuality are increased. For example, stressful experiences are known to result in high levels of stress hormone releasers (such as corticotrophin releasing factor). These activate the adrenal glands to produce other stress hormones known as glucocorti-coids. These hormones have many effects on the body, including the suppression of digestion and immune function, in favour of mobilizing energy resources for emergency action. They also suppress the activity of the testes and ovaries, so these gonads release less of their testosterone or oestrogens, hence it is easy to see how stress in the mother could potentially interfere with normal sexual development. The pathways whereby male or female foetuses differentiate during development might be affected by stress hormones diffusing through the placenta into the foetus.

The theory was bolstered by some laboratory experiments in which pregnant female rats were stressed by confinement (Ward, 1972). The male offspring of these stressed rats tended to show reduced mounting behaviour (a male-typical sexual behaviour) and increased lordosis. Thus it seemed that the rats were de-masculinized (showed reduced mounting) and feminized (showed lordosis). However, the relevance of this animal work is questionable. For example, although prenatal stressors appear to increase the likelihood of lordosis in male rats, the full range of female-typical behaviour is not found. Nor is it clear whether sexual preference itself is affected or just actual sexual performance. Also, there is some debate as to whether there are differences in the hormone profiles of control versus stressed male rats (Ward *et al.*, 2002). Clearly, these data are of limited value when applied to humans. Gay men are not necessarily de-masculinized in their sexual behaviour; mounting is performed about as often as recipient sex, but they are feminized in their direction of sexual preference.

The primary figure for the prenatal stress theory of homosexuality is the German scientist Gunter Dorner (Dorner *et al.*, 1980; 1983). In order to test his idea that stress in pregnant women would predispose her unborn male child (Dorner was silent on lesbians) towards homosexuality, Dorner attempted to find out how many gay men were born during the Second World War compared to peacetime by checking the birth dates of gay men registered with sexual disease doctors in East Germany. Indeed, he found that more gay men were born during the war or the two years following it. In another study he asked gay and straight men about any stressful events that their mothers experienced during pregnancy. The results were rather surprising, as Dorner claimed that around 60 per cent of the mothers of gay men reported moderate to severe stress during pregnancy (mostly war-related stressors, such loss of their husband or rape) whereas only 6 per cent of straight men reported that their mothers suffered such stressful events. The figures seem very high and it is not surprising that later studies have failed to replicate them (e.g. Bailey *et al.*, 1991; Schmidt and Clement,

1995). Mike Bailey's study was perhaps the most methodologically sound. He asked a large number of mothers of gay and heterosexual men about their memories of stressful events during pregnancy and found no differences between the two groups of mums.

More recently, Lee Ellis and Shirley Cole-Harding (2001) of Minot State University reported on 7,500 homosexual and heterosexual offspring and their mothers, who provided retrospective information on their stressful experiences, alcohol use and nicotine use during pregnancy. Ellis and Cole-Harding found that the mothers of gay men reported higher levels of stress during the first and second months of pregnancy in comparison to mothers of straight men. There were no differences relating to stress during any other month of pregnancy. Also, there were no differences in reports of stress between the mothers of lesbian and straight women. The inclusion of measures of substance use (alcohol and nicotine) is again based on animal studies showing atypical sexual behaviour in the offspring of pregnant females administered various drugs. These studies are subject to the same criticisms as those relating to animal studies of prenatal stress. In their human study, Ellis and Cole-Harding found no differences in maternal reports of alcohol consumption between heterosexuals and homosexuals, but the mothers of lesbians reported more cigarette smoking during the first and second months of pregnancy compared to mothers of straight women. Although this study comprised a very large sample overall, the size of homosexual group was much smaller (332 compared to 7,473 heterosexuals). This poses problems for the type of statistical tests the researchers used, so their results should be interpreted cautiously.

In another study (Ellis and Hellberg, 2004) the recollections of 5,102 mothers were taken concerning their use of therapeutic drugs during pregnancy. With respect to male offspring there was no link between prenatal exposure to any medications and sexual orientation. However, the consumption of certain prescription drugs during the first trimester of pregnancy (particularly amphetamine-based diet pills and synthetic thyroxin) was higher for the mothers of lesbians. This work is interesting in suggesting that female sexual orientation may be affected by drug use in the mother. By contrast, most 'stress' theorists have focused on the determination of male homosexuality.

The above studies depend upon accurate retrospective reporting by mothers, which is something of a limitation. The prospective paradigm is obviously preferable, and one such study speaks strongly against the prenatal psychological stress theory. Professor Melissa Hines of City University, London, a leading scientist in the area of sex hormones and behaviour, and colleagues at the University of Bristol examined this issue in a prospective population study of 13,998 pregnancies resulting in 14,138 offspring (Hines *et al.*, 2002). This type of study is methodologically superior because it examines a number of psychological and physical traits from a representative sample of participants and follows the children up at various time points. The researchers sent mothers a questionnaire at 18 weeks of gestation which asked them about the levels of stress they experienced from the onset of pregnancy till 18 weeks, and from week 19 until eight weeks following the child's birth. The children were followed up at 42 months of age and their sex-typical behaviours were assessed using a standard observation instrument called the Pre-School Activities Inventory. This asks mothers to rate the extent to which their child engages with sex-typical toys and games. The researchers found no association between prenatal stress levels and sex-typed behaviour in boys. There was a slight relationship between the two variables in girls but this was of minimal significance. No associations between substance use (nicotine, alcohol and cannabis use) and sex-typed behaviour were found for boys, and the relationships present in girls were again minimal. Now although this study could not look at sexual orientation *per se*, as we shall see in Chapter 8 childhood gender-role behaviour is a very good predictor of adult sexual orientation. All in all, there is little evidence to support the prenatal stress theory of sexual orientation.

Developmental instability

A final competing theory for the development of homosexuality is developmental instability (or DI). DI refers to an organism's level of vulnerability to environmental and genetic stresses during general biological development (Moller and Swaddle, 199; Lalumiere *et al.*, 2000). When applied to sexual orientation this simply means that homosexuality reflects a kind of disruption in the normal biological 'ideal' blueprint of otherwise heterosexual human beings. It is believed that measures of this instability provide some insight into the developmental history of the organism. The best way to measure DI is to measure the right and left sides of various anatomical features of the body, often things like the lengths of the fingers, dermato-glyphics, the lengths of the ears, ankles, feet and wrists. You then subtract the measurement for one side from the other to obtain an absolute difference score. Higher scores indicate greater discrepancy between right and left side measurements and are believed to result when the body plan for the individual is disrupted in some way on either side of the body. This measure is called 'fluctuating asymmetry' (or FA).

If homosexuality results from the foetus's inability to buffer itself against various kinds of environmental and genetic insults, then homosexuals should show greater FA. In fact they do not – neither gay men nor lesbians. Brian Mustanski's study of dermatoglyphic features and sexual orientation found no differences between heterosexuals and homosexuals in the asymmetry of fingerprints (Mustanski *et al.*, 2002). In our own study on finger-length ratios in 240 volunteers we computed a measure of FA by subtracting the right from the left finger lengths and found no differences between homosexuals and heterosexuals (Rahman and Wilson, 2003b; see also Green and Young, 2000). This means that homosexuals are as likely as heterosexuals to withstand developmental problems and have robust genetic buffering systems. In other words, homosexuality is not a 'biological error' in this sense of term.

One other marker of DI is left-handedness or non-right-handedness (if handedness is measured on a continuum). There is some evidence that homosexuals of both sexes are less consistently right-handed than hetero-sexuals. Martin Lalumiere and his colleagues from the Centre for Addiction and Mental Health and University of Toronto analysed all the studies con-ducted on sexual orientation and handedness and concluded that homosexuals of both sexes have a 39 per cent greater chance of being non-right-handed (Lalumiere *et al.*, 2000). Lalumiere and colleagues argue that the patterns of handedness shown by gay men and lesbians reflect the actions of a generalized DI mechanism that shifts erotic preferences away from the species-typical pattern of opposite-sex attraction. But as we have already noted there is no evidence for increased DI in homosexuals on FA measures – the more widely accepted marker of DI. In Chapter 7 we will show that the greater non-right-handedness of homosexuals can be accounted for within the prenatal androgen theory.

The general mechanism proposed by the developmental instability theory is inconsistent with most of the data presented above. It cannot easily account for the mosaic pattern of traits we see in homosexuals and it is too domain-general, failing to specify exactly what development mechanisms are disrupted or 'unstable'. Prenatal androgen theory does, however, show promise of being able to do this.

CHAPTER **SIX**
The big brother effect

I T IS A common view that your birth order – whether you are the first-born, last-born or somewhere in between – influences the way you are treated by your parents and siblings, and thus shapes aspects of your personality. Parents are typically nervous with their first-borns as they are inexperienced and grow in confidence with their subsequent children. Perhaps they transmit this nervousness or confidence to first-born and second-born children respectively. Siblings also appear to interact with their younger or older siblings differently. Various 'happy-family' scenarios come to mind where younger brothers are instructed in sports, fighting, breaking curfews and going on adventures by their older brothers. Older brothers perhaps also offer protection against potential threats in the playground, and younger brothers may come to admire their older brothers as role models. Can older brothers also influence the sexual orientation of their younger brothers? The answer appears to be yes. However, contrary to the common view, this is probably not because of the psychosocial effects of having older brothers but rather the effects of the mother's immune system arising as a result of carrying successive male foetuses during gestation.

The 'fraternal birth order effect'

Inquiries into whether one's birth order could affect sexual orientation began as early as the 1930s. Researchers were interested in the question of whether the average birth order of gay men was particularly early or late. But early research used poor methods and was something of a casual, unserious interest for some psychiatrists and psychologists. For example, the earlier work used a categorical approach to birth order by dividing the birth orders of straight and gay men into 'first-born', 'middle-born' and 'last-born'. This is clearly erroneous as it means that the second of four children will be placed in the same category as the fifth of six children (i.e.

the 'middle-born' category). The result is a loss of specific information about the birth order of the subjects and a considerable reduction in statistical power. However, in around half of these older studies gay men tended to have a later birth order than straight men (e.g. Martensen-Larsen, 1957; Schofield, 1965).

The psychiatrist Elliot Slater of the Maudsley Hospital in London devised a quantitative measure of birth order that was more sensitive because it did not involve categorizing birth order. This is called 'Slater's Index' and is computed simply by dividing the number of older siblings by the total number of siblings. This produces a number between 0 and 1, where 0 corresponds to first-born and 1 to last-born. This is not the only way to quantify birth order but it is the most widely used formula. Slater conducted his own studies on birth order and sexual orientation and found a Slater score of 0.58 in a sample of 337 gay men who were patients at the Maudsley Hospital (Slater, 1962). This was greater than the expected value of 0.50, indicating that gay men had a later birth order than that theoretically expected for the general population. Unfortunately, Slater had no heterosexual comparison group, which is important because family sizes change over the years, causing variations in the expected value of 0.50.

The researcher who has made the greatest contribution to this field by far is Ray Blanchard, who is head of the clinical sexology programme at the Centre for Addiction and Mental Health in Toronto. He and his colleagues began to examine the question of birth order and sexual orientation in a series of studies that used heterosexual control groups and also non-clinical samples of gay men. Typically, studies by this group and others recruit large numbers of gay and straight men and ask them to identify every child carried by their mother (as far as possible including foetuses that were miscarried). These are ranked in terms of birth order so that the gender and numbers of older and younger siblings born to their mothers can be determined precisely. Volunteers are also asked other questions such as their parents' age at their birth. The work by Blanchard and his group using 14 samples totalling over 7,000 individuals in several countries spanning several decades shows consistently that gay men are born later than heterosexual men (a review of the data up to around 1997 can be found in Blanchard, 1997; for subsequent studies see also Blanchard, 2001; Blanchard, 2004).

Finding the same results in 14 out of 14 studies is unlikely to be down to chance, so we can say with confidence that the birth order effect in human sexual orientation is real. But the more interesting question is whether it arises because gay men have more siblings of one sex or the other. As Blanchard notes, the sexual orientation of a newborn boy cannot operate backwards in time to affect his number of older siblings, thus the number of older siblings, or some factors related to it, must affect the newborn's sexual orientation. As was said earlier, birth order studies ask the volunteers about the number and sex of each of the probands' siblings. Ray Blanchard and Anthony Bogaert (1996a) asked these questions of 302 gay men and 302 straight men recruited in Ontario, Canada, who were matched on year of birth. They found that the gay men had significantly more older brothers (an average of 1.31 compared with 0.96 for straight men). However, the number of older sisters, younger brothers and younger sisters bore no relationship to sexual orientation, and neither did parental age or the interval between births. Thus what seems to be critical is the number of older brothers and not any other type of sibling. This is why the finding is called the fraternal birth order effect. The effect has been replicated time and time again in many countries, in psychiatric and non-psychiatric samples of men, in the Kinsey data archives, in large-scale national probability samples (thus eliminating ascertainment biases), in men who want to become women (transsexuals), in adolescent gay boys and in boys who wish they were girls (e.g. Blanchard et al., 1995; Blanchard and Bogaert, 1996b; Bogaert, 1998b; Jones and Blanchard, 1998; Green, 2000; Purcell et al., 2000; Ellis and Blanchard, 2001; Bogaert, 2003; Poasa et al., 2004). The effect is even stronger in very feminine gay men (Blanchard and Sheridan, 1992) and also predicts bachelorhood (unmarried men being more likely to have gay brothers as well as a greater number of older brothers in one study: Blanchard and Bogaert, 1997). Blanchard has calculated that the odds of being gay increase by around 33 per cent with each older brother (Blanchard and Bogaert, 1996a; see also Bogaert, 2003). Thus the more sons a woman has borne, the greater the likelihood that her subsequent sons will be gay. The fraternal birth order effect is one of the most reliable correlates of male sexual orientation.

In complete contrast, female sexual orientation is totally unaffected by birth order or sibling sex composition. The number of older brothers (or any other class of sibling, for that matter) a woman has makes no difference to whether she will turn out to be a lesbian or not. For example, Anthony Bogaert examined the Kinsey data archives for birth order information for 257 lesbian women and 5,008 heterosexual women and found no birth order effect or differences in sibling sex composition (Bogaert, 1997). Other studies confirm that females do not influence their siblings' sexual orientation and siblings do not influence theirs (Blanchard *et al.*, 1998; Ellis and Blanchard, 2001). Thus the fraternal birth order effect is specific to male sexual orientation, and does not affect female sexual orientation. Any theory seeking to explain it will need to take this sex difference into account.

How many brothers does it take to make you gay?

The fraternal birth order effect in male homosexuality clearly contributes to the 'non-shared' environmental component of sexual orientation, that is the variance not accounted for either by genetics or by environmental forces that are shared by members of the same family (see Chapter 3). By definition, your birth order is a way in which you differ from your siblings. The next question to ask is how important the effect is in male sexual orientation. Blanchard felt compelled to address this question because the popular media suggested that some parents (perhaps homophobic ones) might be inclined to abort male foetuses after they had already produced two or three sons for fear of adding future gay sons to their families. Fortunately, the fraternal birth order effect is not so strong that it would tempt parents to unsavoury family planning of this kind. Blanchard used some mathematics to show that if we assume a population base rate of homosexuality in men with no older brothers at around 2 per cent, and then factor in the odds of each older brother increasing the chances of subsequent brothers being gay by 33 per cent, the probability that a couple's son will be gay rises from 2 per cent for their first son to 6 per cent by their fifth son. Although this is a threefold increase, there remains a 94 per cent likelihood that the fifth son will be heterosexual (Blanchard, 2001). Thus the tactic of aborting male foetuses for the purpose of eliminating gay sons would result in the elimination of a great many more heterosexual sons.

This leaves us with the question of how strong the fraternal birth order effect really is in gay men. In other words, how many gay men owe their sexual orientation to the big brother effect? Blanchard and his colleague

James Cantor worked this out using some mathematical procedures from the science of epidemiology in a community sample of 302 gay men and 302 straight men. Their conclusion was that about one in seven gay men owed their sexual orientation to the big brother effect (Cantor *et al.*, 2002). A boy with two and a half older brothers is twice as likely to be gay as a boy with no older brothers, and a boy with four older brothers is three times as likely to be gay. Also, the effect of fraternal birth order would exceed all other causes of homosexuality in men with three or more older brothers. In a further analysis using large, representative US and UK samples, Blanchard and Bogaert (2004) reported that around 28 per cent of gay men owed their sexual orientation to their fraternal birth order. Overall, these results show that a substantial proportion (but clearly not all) of gay men owe their sexuality to fraternal birth order.

These results have implications for some of the genetic research on homosexuality discussed in Chapter 3. Recall that not all genetic studies found genetic markers for sexual orientation, and these studies use gay brother pairs as their staple sample. Factoring in fraternal birth order may shed light on some of the reasons for the difficulty in finding genetic linkage. Since gay brother pairs, other than identical twins, contain one brother who is older than the other, the fraternal birth order effect predicts that the younger brother would have increased odds of being gay (by virtue of having an older brother). Depending on the precise model used to calculate the genetic effect, this could either enhance or obscure it.

Having established that a fraternal birth order effect exists for male sexual orientation (and there are really no two ways about it), we need to ask how and why. As was pointed out earlier, a man's homosexuality cannot operate backwards in time to provide him with older brothers, so either the presence of older brothers somehow promotes a homosexual preference in the younger son, or a third factor causes the association. One theory is that the number of older brothers in a man's social environment (outside of the womb) produces homosexuality. The second (and much more likely) explanation is that prenatal events related to the fact that a gay man's mother has carried a number of prior male foetuses (whether or not they result in live births) cause his homosexuality.

Social environment and the big brother effect – is there a link?

As mentioned above, it is a common view that parents treat their children differently depending on the order in which they are born. Parents of first-borns are anxious with their first child because they are unrehearsed in parenting skills and afraid they might get it wrong. The first child also begins with total parental attention, but much of this is diverted to the cuter and cuddlier new arrivals. First-borns might be given more responsibility and restricted in their independence by parents. If parents treat their first-borns differently from second-borns then we should find a birth order effect on children's personalities. Perhaps these personality differences result in different sexualities and thus we would expect birth order effects for sexuality.

A favourite psychosocial theory of the origin of homosexuality – putting it down to a smothering, over-attentive mother – would predict more homosexuality in first-borns than later-borns, since presumably they get more parental attention. This, of course, is the reverse of what is actually observed in the fraternal birth order data. In any case, the view that birth order affects personality in children has scant support. Psychologists have spent decades searching for birth order effects in personality and have found none that are at all robust or reliable. Judy Dunn (an expert in sibling relationships) and Robert Plomin (a leading figure in behaviour genetics) looked carefully at the birth order data and found no convincing effects (Dunn and Plomin, 1990). Similarly, a review of studies published from 1946 to 1980 by Cecile Ernst and Jules Angst found no consistent birth order effects on personality. Their own research with over 7,000 volunteers also found no differences between first-borns and second-borns in several personality traits (Ernst and Angst, 1983).

Any theory proposing that personality influences sexuality thus founders on the fact that there are no reliable birth order effects on personality in the first place. Some have proposed, for example, that later-born children develop feelings of inadequacy or make negative self-comparisons in relation to older siblings and these may predispose towards homosexuality in later-borns. There is no evidence that feelings of inadequacy (whatever that means exactly) predispose towards homosexuality. Even if there was, there might be a confusion of cause and effect, with homosexuals feeling inadequate within a society which stigmatizes them. A version of this idea was suggested by Daryl Bem (1996) in his 'Exotic Becomes Erotic' theory of sexual orientation (Chapter 2). Bem suggested that feminine boys feel different from more masculine boys and this feeling of difference leads to eroticization of other males. Bem argues that having more older brothers would increase these feelings of difference such that the feminine boy would be even more likely to be attracted to males. Unfortunately, Bem's theory uses the same mechanism to account for lesbianism and would therefore predict that lesbians would have more older sisters (which they do not).

Another theory suggests that mothers with many sons would be inclined to hanker for a girl in the family and thus tend to treat one of their later sons as one. This idea would predict that gay men would show a lack of older sisters as well as more older brothers. The fraternal birth order data reviewed earlier shows no such deficit in sisters in gay probands' families, so there is no reason for mothers to feel they lack daughters. Thus none of the above psychosocial theories can be reconciled with the big brother effect as it is actually observed.

By far the most popular psychosocial theory for the fraternal birth order effect in male sexual orientation is the idea that sexual interaction with older males increases a boy's probability of developing a homosexual orientation and that a boy's chances of engaging in such interactions increases with the more older brothers he has. Frank Sulloway in his book *Born to Rebel* argues that later-borns are more 'open to experience' and thus more likely to explore homosexual activity compared to early-born boys, which may result in a stable homosexual orientation in adulthood. As we have shown in Chapter 2, there is no evidence to support a role for contagion or seduction in the origins of sexual orientation. Incestuous sex play between brothers, or early homosexual experimentation among boys (say in boarding school), does not *cause* homosexual orientation in later adult life, even though it usually precedes it. So the theory is already a non-starter.

Further evidence from the birth order literature puts another coffin nail into this theory. Anthony Bogaert examined the large US national probability sample by Laumann *et al.* (1994) for data on sexual orientation, birth order and sibling sexual activity and found the standard birth order effect for gay men (Bogaert, 2000). But Bogaert went on to demonstrate that sibling sexual activity did not underlie the association between birth order and homosexuality. In further work with two national probability samples, Bogaert (2003) tested a prediction derived from Sulloway's theory that the number of older brothers should relate more strongly to early same-sex experience than to same-sex attraction. He found that the fraternal birth order effect was strongly related to homosexual attraction (i.e. the 'core' of what sexual orientation is, as discussed in Chapter 1) but not to behaviour (the mediating factor according to Sulloway's theory). Same-sex experience was not related to number of older brothers, and the fraternal birth order effect was completely unrelated to same-sex behaviour, including early same-sex experiences. We may therefore conclude with some degree of certainty that the big brother effect on male sexual orientation has nothing to do with living with older brothers, learning or family dynamics.

The mother's immune system

How do we know that the fraternal birth order effect influences sexual orientation before birth? One observation that points to this conclusion is that birth weight is affected by the number of older brothers – boys who have lots of older brothers weigh less at birth than boys who have the same number of older sisters. Because birth weight is clearly a prenatal phenomenon, a link between birth weight, sexual orientation and number of older brothers would suggest a prenatal determinant for both the fraternal birth order effect and sexual orientation itself. Such a link is exactly what Ray Blanchard and his colleagues have found. Blanchard and Lee Ellis studied 3,229 homosexual and heterosexual men and women whose mothers were able to report on the sex of every child they had previously carried, and gathered information on birth weight and other variables (Blanchard and Ellis, 2001). As anticipated, both straight and gay men with older brothers tended to weigh less than those with older sisters. But, importantly, gay men with older brothers weighed on average 170 grams less at birth than did straight men with older brothers. Gay and straight men with no older brothers, or older sisters only, did not differ in birth weight. The researchers confirmed this finding in 250 effeminate boys (feminine childhood behaviour being predictive of adult homosexuality in men). Those with two or more older brothers weighed 385 grams less at birth than control (non-effeminate) boys with two or more older brothers (Blanchard *et al.*, 2002). Thus it seems that the events by which older brothers increase the odds of homosexuality in later-born males – factors relating to the mother's previous male pregnancies – operate before birth.

Blanchard and Bogaert (1996a; see also Blanchard and Klassen, 1997) have proposed the main theory for high fraternal birth order among gay men. This focuses on the fact that although a foetus cannot know how many brothers were present in the womb before him, the mother's body can, by way of her immune system. The mother's immune system keeps track of how many male foetuses she has carried previously and produces a response in the form of antibodies that attack the intruder. This is precisely what immune systems do – they remember what they have come in contact with and form a response if required. Male foetuses may trigger a reaction in their mothers because they produce hormones or proteins that threaten the mother's balance of sex hormones via placental blood connections. Female foetuses, of course, produce no such biological material that could conflict with the mother's.

This hypothesized mechanism is similar to that recognized in Rhesus blood factor incompatibility. If a mother with blood factor Rh negative (Rh–) carries a child who is Rh positive (Rh+), which she usually does if her partner is Rh+ (this being genetically dominant), she may develop an immune response that affects subsequent Rh+ foetuses. The Rh incompatibility problem is progressive, such that eventually it may be necessary to transfuse the blood of later-born children.

Some mothers, then, may become immunized to a substance important to the development of male foetuses, and this immune response would affect later male pregnancies more strongly. Why the immune system of some mothers might do this is unknown, but it could have something to do with the fact that sons are physiologically more demanding to produce than daughters. Relative to daughters, giving birth to sons is known to reduce maternal longevity, at least in pre-industrial societies (Helle *et al.*, 2002). Also, substances from a female foetus will tend to be recognized as 'self' (i.e. as another female) by the maternal immune system, rather than the more 'alien' or 'non-self' male foetus. Perhaps during evolution females developed an antagonistic immune system to keep in check the number of male foetuses to offset the detrimental consequences of carrying them.

The H-Y antigen

One male-specific substance that might trigger off a maternal immune attack is the minor histocompatibility antigen known as H-Y. This is found only in males, being produced by genes on the Y chromosome. The H-Y antigen may get into the mother's circulation and set off the mother's alarm bells, triggering her immune system to produce antibodies to H-Y. The H-Y antigens are present in most tissues from very early on, so even if the foetus does make it to term the mother's body is still capable of remembering its existence. Each additional male the mother carries would boost the response, like having a 'booster' injection to increase the immune response against a troublesome virus. Hence the more males the mother carries the stronger her immune response will be. Because sexual differentiation of the brain does not take place till much later in pregnancy the accumulating H-Y antibodies may shift male-typical sexual differentiation in the female-typical direction, giving rise to a homosexual orientation in later-born sons.

The H-Y antigen almost certainly plays a role in sexual differentiation of the brain as its receptors are strongly represented on the surfaces of neurons (brain cells). That makes it very easy for maternal antibodies to target the male foetal brain and influence the development of brain centres controlling sexuality, among other things. It could also mean that, while the brain is affected, others aspects of male-typical development (such as male-typical genitalia) would remain more or less unaffected, since H-Y is less strongly represented in these tissues. It seems that male foetuses are more likely to provoke maternal immune reactions because there are higher levels of antibodies in their blood and in their mothers'. Male foetuses are more likely to elicit maternal Rh immune responses than are female foetuses (Gualtieri and Hicks, 1985; Blanchard and Klassen, 1997). Studies in mice show that around 90 per cent of the male offspring of female mice actively immunized against foetal H-Y show poor reproductive performance, although it is unclear whether this reflects lack of interest, preference or actual sexual behaviour (Singh and Verma, 1987).

Interestingly, the maternal immune hypothesis could explain the birth weight findings discussed a little earlier. Animal studies show that maternal immunization can produce decreases in birth weight, yet increases in the weight of the placenta (e.g. Zuckerman and Head, 1985). Michel Vernier studied over 7,500 human placentas and found that, despite lower birth weight, later-born males had larger placentas than normal (Vernier, 1975). These data suggest that either the mother or the foetus might be attempting to defend against immunologic attack, and development of a larger placenta might be a way of doing this. It is important to remember that there are alternatives to the H-Y antigens which may be involved in maternal immunity responses. For example, Y-linked proteins called protocadherin and neuroligin (which may influence the way neurons in male brains communicate with each other) could also elicit immune responses, or maternal cytokines (which are protein molecules secreted by immune system cells which regulate the immune response) may also cross the placental barrier and affect foetal brain development (Blanchard, 2004).

Although the maternal immune response theory is a powerful explanation of the fraternal birth order effect, it is not without its limitations. Primary among these is the lack of any direct evidence for the role of maternal immune responses in homosexual men compared to heterosexual men. This is not really a fault with the theory; rather we are awaiting the research. Studies will need to examine maternal antibody levels of the mothers of gay and straight men that have older brothers and those that do not. Another limitation is that it can only account for male sexual orientation, although this is a natural consequence of the data, since there is no birth order effect for female sexual orientation, and the type of sibling makes no difference in women. The theory would also predict that brothers born after the gay male proband should also be gay, but there is no available support for this hypothesis. On the contrary, one 'type' of homosexual (male transsexuals who are gay as defined by their genetic sex) shows no departure from a heterosexual orientation in younger brothers (Green, 2000).

Although Green's findings appear to contradict the maternal immunization theory, they might be explained by differing 'vulnerability' of the foetus to maternal immune responses (Blanchard, 2004). For example, genetic factors (Chapter 3) could produce differential sensitivity. This illustrates an important point: genetics cannot account for everything, any more than birth order can, but each might be responsible for the sexual orientation of some gay men. The fact that there were no differences in birth weight between first-born gay and heterosexual men, or between gay and heterosexual men who only had older sisters, suggests that gay men with no older brothers must acquire their sexual orientation through other biological means. These could include specific types of gay genes and differential exposure to prenatal androgens (or some interaction between these two).

The key point arising from the last few chapters is that, whether it results from purely genetic factors, prenatal androgen effects or (more likely) an interaction between the two, sexual orientation (both straight and gay) is a matter that is pretty much settled well before birth.

CHAPTER **SEVEN**
The gay brain

In the preceding chapters we have considered some of the genetic and prenatal mechanisms by which sexual orientation may arise. Clearly, whatever the precise mechanism, these influences must have their effects on the developing brain of the 'pre-heterosexual' or 'pre-homosexual' individual forming in the womb. After all, it is the brain that generates all our behaviour (not some wisp behind our heads called 'the mind' which we carry with us like a balloon), and it is an understated cliché that this is the greatest sexual organ we possess!

Genetic and prenatal determinants of sexual orientation presumably influence how the nerve cells grow and connect with each other in specific parts of the brain that control direction of sexual preference to make one person attracted to the opposite sex and another person attracted to the same sex. Prenatal hormones or maternal antibodies could do this through interacting with sex hormone receptors, or alternatively 'gay genes' could be preferentially 'transcribed' directly in the brain independent of hormone effects. In this chapter we look at the documented sexual-orientation-related differences in the structure and function of the brain and consider the various clues as to how sexual preferences originate and are neurologically coded.

The hypothalamus

An area called the hypothalamus (Figure 7.1) appears to be a key sex centre in mammals. It is a small region located in the base of the brain and consists of right and left halves separated by a fluid-filled cavity in the middle of the brain called the third ventricle. It also has several areas, such as the anterior (front) part, the posterior (back) part, the ventromedial (underside-middle) area, the medial preoptic (close to the crossing of the visual pathways) area and others. It is certainly not the only region that controls sexuality, and it does not work in isolation. There is more likely a network or circuit of brain regions (in which the hypothalamus is key) responsible for sexuality, involving other structures, such as the amygdala, as well as 'higher' cortical regions. Areas within the hypothalamus may control different aspects of sexuality, but there is still debate as to whether it controls most or all aspects of sexuality (preference for males or females, sexual motivation, approach behaviour and sexual performance) or simply a few of these aspects. Apart from its role in sexuality, the hypothalamus is also involved with other important functions such as eating, drinking and temperature regulation.

Figure 7.1. A vertical slice of the human brain taken from an MRI image showing the approximate location of the hypothalamus.

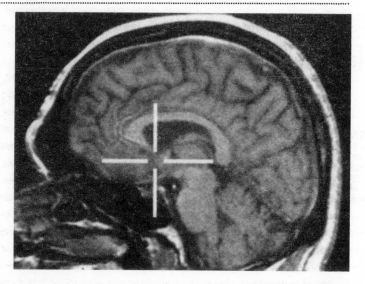

We know that the regions of the hypothalamus are involved in various aspects of sexuality from studies in laboratory animals, mostly rats, but also in primates. In males the medial preoptic area is involved in male-typical sexual behaviour such as mounting, intromission and ejaculation, and may also be involved in sexual preference as well. Damage to this area causes a reduction in these male-typical sexual behaviours. In females damage to another region called the ventromedial nucleus produces deficits in female-typical sexual behaviour such as lordosis. Researchers at Boston University have demonstrated that destroying various parts of the medial preoptic area produces a female-typical pattern of approach behaviour in male ferrets such that they prefer another male ferret to a receptive female when given a choice (Paredes and Baum, 1995; Kindon *et al.*, 1996). In male primates damage to the medial preoptic area results in a reduction of interest in heterosexual partners, although there is no increase in homosexual activity.

Importantly, a group of neurons (a nucleus) within the medial preoptic area show sexual dimorphism, a difference between males and females. In rats this nucleus is known as the sexually dimorphic nucleus of the preoptic area (SDN-POA). This was discovered by Roger Gorski and his team at UCLA to be around eight times larger in male than in female rats (Gorski *et al.*, 1978). Sexual dimorphisms in similar nuclei have also been found in other mammals, such as guinea pigs, ferrets, sheep (which we discuss later) and some primates. The main cause of this sex difference (as with most other physical sex differences) appears to be the differing exposure of males and females to testosterone in the womb (see Chapter 5). Roger Gorski and his team have shown that the sexual dimorphism in the SDN-POA is a direct consequence of differing androgen levels during prenatal development. A female rat could be induced to form a male-sized SDN-POA by injection of testosterone, and male rats could have their SDN-POA reduced to a female size by having their key source of testosterone (their own testes) removed by castration (Davis *et al.*, 1995). Of course, this treatment also causes cross-sex shifts in sexual behaviour, as mentioned earlier. Importantly, this hormone manipulation needs to be done during a critical period of development, in the case of rats a few days before birth or very soon after birth. Any later (e.g. a week after birth) and the hormone manipulations have no effects. Neither can administration of the relevant male-typical or female-typical hormones later after birth 'restore' the size of the SDN-POA to its male-typical or female-typical size. In other words, male sex hormones organize the structure of the SDN-POA during early prenatal life and cannot be altered by changes in hormone levels after birth or in adulthood. It is likely that the testosterone effect on the SDN-POA acts within the male brain through conversion to oestrogen via aromatase (see Chapter 5), since males treated with aromatase inhibitor also develop the female-typical SDN-POA (Houtsmuller *et al.*, 1994).

Strangely, in rats the structure that appears to control female sexual behaviour, the ventromedial nucleus, shows no obvious sex difference, although another structure called the anteroventral periventricular nucleus (AVPV, located at the tip of the hypothalamus) is larger in females than males. This is most probably because it is implicated in the regulation of the rat equivalent of the menstrual cycle. Prenatal testosterone levels also influence the structure of the AVPV such that higher levels cause a smaller nucleus, the very opposite of what happens to the SDN-POA. Thus it seems that the brain differences related to female sexual behaviour are more subtle and complex than they are in males.

Studies in humans have located an equivalent of the SDN-POA. In 1989 Gorski's group (led by his student Laura Allen) examined the hypothalamus from brains obtained at autopsy. They discovered two nuclei in the anterior hypothalamus called INAH-2 and INAH-3 (INAH meaning the interstitial nuclei of the anterior hypothalamus) that were larger in men than in women (see Figure 7.2). The sex difference for INAH-2 was less clear, but the difference for INAH-3 was marked – males having almost three times as large an INAH-3 as women (Allen *et al.*, 1989). The sex difference for INAH-3, but not INAH-2, has been independently verified, so seems to be fairly robust (LeVay, 1991; Byne *et al.*, 2000; Byne *et al.*, 2001). The location of INAH-3, its structure and chemical composition are similar to that of the rat SDN-POA, suggesting that the two structures are 'homologous' and probably have the same origins and functions across various mammals (Byne, 1998). There are also sex differences in several other human brain structures that are implicated in sexual behaviour (e.g. the amygdala and bed nucleus of the stria terminalis), but no studies have explored whether these also vary by sexual orientation.

Oddly, the first reported difference in the hypothalamic region between heterosexual and homosexual men was not for the INAH, but for a group of cells called the supra-chiasmatic nucleus (SCN). This area is in fact primarily concerned with controlling the sleep–waking cycle of many animals, including humans. Nonetheless it is also involved in the control of reproductive behaviour in animals across daily and seasonal cycles. The Dutch brain researcher Dick Swaab and his colleagues at the Netherlands Institute for Brain Research reported that the size of the SCN was larger, and its shape longer, in gay men than in heterosexual men, a configuration more characteristic of women (Swaab and Hofman, 1990). Interestingly, the size difference was specific to a population of cells called arginine vasopressin neurons (AVP), which are implicated in the sleep–waking cycle of humans. Studies with rats also suggest SCN involvement in sexual preference; males treated with aromatase inhibitor (disrupting the conversion of testosterone to oestrogen and thus leaving the brain partially feminized since this pathway is important to the normal process of masculinization) become 'bisexual' and show an increased number of AVP neurons in the SCN (Swaab *et al.*, 1995). One preliminary report found a functional significance for the sexual orientation difference, gay men and lesbians appearing to have different sleep–waking patterns compared to heterosexual men and women (Rahman and Silber, 2000). However, this could have resulted from lifestyle differences between heterosexuals and homosexuals (for example, gay men and lesbians staying out later in the evening than heterosexuals, or vice versa). Hence the jury is still out on what the SCN differences might mean. Also, no one has yet replicated the difference reported by Swaab and Hofman.

Figure 7.2. Cross-section of the hypothalamus region showing the major nuclei where some sex- and sexual-orientation-related differences have been shown.

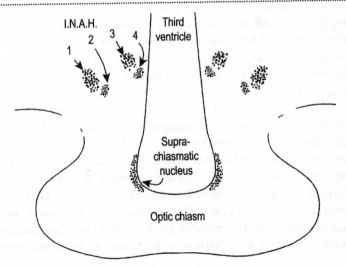

Returning to the INAH, here we have perhaps the best-known report for a sexual orientation difference. Simon LeVay (then of the Salk Institute in San Diego) examined the INAHs of gay men, straight men and straight women in autopsy brain tissue. Since INAH-3 differs between men and women, LeVay wondered if gay men might have a female-like INAH-3. LeVay first confirmed the sex difference in INAH-3 (as detailed above), then went on to observe that gay men had a smaller INAH-3 than straight men. In fact it was comparable in size to that of straight women (LeVay, 1991). LeVay had used autopsy tissue primarily from people who had died of AIDS-related conditions (that is how he established their sexual orientation – it was written in their medical records). However, it is unlikely that AIDS influenced the result as the difference between gay and straight men held up when the gay men were compared to straight men who had also died from complications of AIDS.

More recent work attempting to replicate LeVay's findings has produced less striking results. William Byne and his colleagues from the Mount Sinai School of Medicine in New York obtained autopsy brain material from 34 straight men (24 who were HIV negative and ten HIV positive), 34 straight women (25 were HIV negative and nine HIV positive) and 14 HIV-positive gay men. Byne confirmed that INAH-3 was larger in straight men than in straight women, but found only a trend towards a smaller INAH-3 in gay men that was not statistically reliable. Nor were there any sexual orientation differences in other sexually dimorphic features of INAH-3 (Byne *et al.*, 2001). So the best we can say about the size of INAH-3 is that it is certainly bigger in straight men than in straight women, and might be smaller in gay men, but this difference is not very great at all (Figure 7.3).

Other evidence implicating the hypothalamus in sexual orientation comes from studies of brain responses to erotic stimuli. The hypothalamus is activated more strikingly in straight men than in straight women when they view sexual (as compared with non-sexual) films (Karama *et al.*, 2002). A study using a brain scanning technique called Positron Emission Tomography (or PET) also suggests a hypothalamic difference between heterosexuals and homosexuals. Leann Kinnunen and her colleagues at the University of Chicago examined the brain metabolism of eight gay men and eight straight men and found the straight men to show a significantly stronger response in the hypothalamus to the administration of Fluoxetine, a drug commonly called Prozac (Kinnunen *et al.*, 2003). As Fluoxetine is a drug which stops the reuptake of the brain's 'happy' chemical, serotonin, Kinnunen's study suggests that this neurotransmitter chemical may mediate the activity of the hypothalamus determining male sexual preference.

Figure 7.3. Comparison of the volumetric findings of two autopsy studies of INAH-3 and sexual orientation (data from LeVay, 1991; Byne *et al.*, 2001).

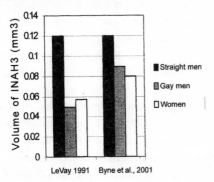

In Chapter 5 we discussed a number of possible hormonal pathways that might produce brain differences affecting whether a person will be attracted to men or women. Which of these pathways could be responsible for the brain differences reported above? One pathway could be the 'androgen receptor' route, in which the androgen receptors (ARs) of the hypothalamus are not as sensitive to the effects of male sex hormones in gay men as they are in heterosexual men, or there simply are not enough of them in gay men in the first place. Compared with women, men do show a greater distribution of ARs in areas of the hypothalamus, such as one called the mamillary body complex (or MBC) (Fernandez-Guasti *et al.*, 2000). However, Frank Kruijver and colleagues from the Netherlands Institute for Brain Research found no variation in ARs between the post-mortem brains of young straight and gay men – at least in the MBC (Kruijver *et al.*, 2001). This links with the findings of Macke *et al.* (1993), discussed in Chapter 3, showing no association between homosexuality and AR sequence variation. The second idea – that gay men might not differ in the distribution of ARs, but in the responsivity of ARs to testosterone – is supported by the work on people with Complete Androgen Insensitivity Syndrome (see Chapter 5). Unfortunately, no studies have examined normal heterosexual and gay men.

Another pathway, this time focusing on the aromatase to oestrogen road of male sexual differentiation, has rather more support. Men show higher aromatase activity than women in the medial preoptic regions of the hypothalamus (Fernandez-Guasti *et al.*, 2000). Rodent models confirm that a larger SCN-AVP complex (as shown by gay men) can be induced by blocking aromatase activity and thus reducing metabolism of testosterone to oestrogen (Bakker and Slob, 1997). Further evidence for the role of aromatase and oestrogen receptors in the differentiation of male sexual orientation comes from studies of male-oriented, or homosexual, sheep (Roselli *et al.*, 2004). Around 8 per cent of rams show sexual preference for other rams and no interest in oestrus ewes, yet there are no deficits in other aspects of their sexual functioning. Importantly, sheep also have a sexually dimorphic group of neurons in the medial preoptic areas of their hypothalamus, called the Ovine Sexually Dimorphic Nucleus (oSDN), which is bigger in rams than in ewes. Charles Roselli and his colleagues at the Oregon Health and Science University and the United States Sheep Experiment Station have found that the brains of homosexual rams show smaller oSDNs than heterosexual rams. These researchers also conducted fine-grained neurochemical analyses of these brains, detecting reduced distributions of oestrogen receptors in the amygdala and less aromatase activity in the oSDN of homosexual rams compared with heterosexual rams (Roselli *et al.*, 2004). This profile is similar to that found in ewes.

Thus far, the INAH-3 findings, neuroimaging and animal work all suggest a role for the hypothalamus in the sexual attraction component of sexual orientation. Experiments in several species also show that the development of sexually dimorphic nuclei within the medial preoptic area of the anterior hypothalamus (such as the oSDN of sheep) are the direct result of exposure to prenatal testosterone or its metabolites during the early prenatal (or very early postnatal, depending on the species) period (Cooke *et al.*, 1998). It is important to remember that the size differences could mean a number of different things. They might reflect differences in the connections between neurons, the neurochemical content of neurons, the expression of certain genes within these nuclei, or possibly even the extent to which the circuitry has been 'used'. For example, it could be argued that something about having gay sex (or heterosexual sex for that matter) produces the differences in brain structure. So far all the studies in humans have used gay men, straight men and straight women, but not lesbian women. Hence we know much less about the neural basis of lesbianism.

Lesbianism and the limbic system

One study by our group does shed light on the possible brain basis for sexual orientation in women. We (Rahman, Kumari and Wilson, 2003) have discovered sexual-orientation-related differences between straight and lesbian women in a brain 'circuit' called the cortico-pallido-striato-thalamic circuit, which is primarily based in the limbic region. This has been gleaned from a study of a phenomenon called pre-pulse inhibition of the startle response (PPI), which originates from this brain circuit. PPI refers to a well-recognized reduction in the startle response (usually indexed by the strength of the eye-blink response) to a strong sensory stimulus if preceded by a weak stimulus – the pre-pulse. This measure is interesting because there are reliable sex differences, in both humans and animals, with lower PPIs being shown by females than males.

We sought to examine sexual orientation differences, using a sample of 15 straight men, 15 gay men, 15 straight women and 14 lesbian women. All participants were exposed to a series of loud 'scratching' noises presented in pulses, which would occasionally be preceded by quieter noises, through headphones in a dimly lit room with no external distractions. Eye-blink responses to these sounds were recorded using electrodes attached under the right eye. Not only did we observe the expected sex difference between straight men and women but lesbians were similar to men in terms of their PPIs. There was also a tendency towards female-like responding in gay men, although this was not statistically significant. As PPI is non-learned, and shows parallels across many species (including invertebrates such as water molluscs), these differences implicate 'hard-wiring' in limbic brain circuitry in the determination of female sexual orientation. Our findings are also consistent with previously reported differences in auditory neural circuits reported by Dennis McFadden and colleagues in their study of auditory evoked potentials (see Chapter 5).

Cognitive abilities

Further evidence for brain differences between heterosexuals and homosexuals can be gleaned from looking at how well they perform on certain types of mental abilities that are known to depend on the integrity of certain brain regions. Often these abilities are called cognitive, neuropsychological or neurocognitive to emphasize the link between ability and a brain region.

For many years it has been recognized that there are reliable sex differences on certain types of cognitive tests. Men are usually better able to turn objects around in their imagination, a skill called mental rotation (e.g. rotating a three-dimensional object to match its pair; see Figure 7.4). They are also better at perceiving and judging spatial relationships (e.g. judging the orientation of lines; see Figure 7.5), targeting and intercepting objects that are moving in a trajectory (in other words, throwing and catching accurately) and finding their way about in novel environments (exemplified in map reading). Men appear to be good at navigating because they use cardinal directions and distances pictured from a 'bird's-eye' perspective (a 'Euclidean' strategy); women navigate more in relation to verbally tagged landmarks (e.g. 'Go past the church and turn left at the Safeways'). The importance of male skills to their presumed evolutionary specialization (exploring, hunting and fighting) is evident.

Of course, men are not superior in all respects. Women typically perform better than men on tests of 'verbal fluency' (e.g. producing as many words as they can think of beginning with a particular group of letters or belonging to a category such as 'fruit'). They are better at rapidly matching figures to numbers (coding and perceptual speed), remembering the locations of objects previously seen but then hidden away (a different kind of spatial ability called object location memory; see Figure 7.6). They also excel in various social and communicative abilities, such as reading emotion in faces and understanding other people's feelings (often called female intuition and empathy). Such skills fit well with the traditional female roles of teacher, nurse and oiler of the social cogs, and would account for the pre-eminence of women in certain professions, such as simultaneous translation and the writing of romantic novels.

Figure 7.4. Examples of a spatial rotation task: are the two objects the same or different?

Figure 7.5. Example of a line orientation task: identify these angles according to the key below.

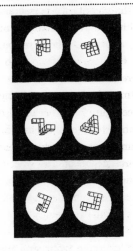

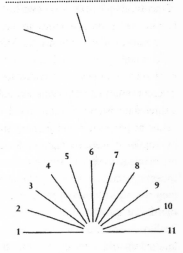

Figure 7.6 Example of an array of objects used in a test of object location memory. After studying the board for a short time, the objects are removed and the subject attempts to replace them in the original positions.

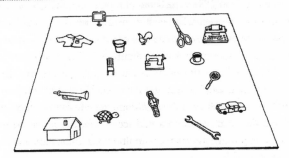

Although some psychologists continue to protest that these sexually dimorphic ability profiles are learned rather than biological, their arguments are not persuasive. The social learning explanation might seem plausible with respect to men and women in our society but similar differences have been observed in all societies, modern and historic, as well as many non-human mammalian species. There is also some direct evidence that sex differences in cognitive abilities arise from differences in levels of prenatal sex hormones. For example, studies in women with CAH (Chapter 5) show enhanced performance on male-typical abilities such as targeted throwing, but not other abilities. The literature on this question has been well reviewed by Doreen Kimura from Simon Fraser University, the leading figure on sex differences in cognition and its causes, in her accessible book *Sex and Cognition* (1999).

So do gay men think like straight men or more like women, and do lesbian women think like straight women or more like men? The answers are by no means clear-cut, but there is a considerable degree of cross-over. A series of studies by ourselves (and other laboratories) has revealed that gay men show fairly consistent female-like performance on male-typical tests such as mental rotation and tests of spatial perception. In our study of 240 healthy heterosexual and homosexual men and women (60 per group), we found large differences between straight and gay men (with straights outperforming gays) on mental rotation and judgement of line orientation. We also found that gay men outperformed straight men by a large margin on the female-typical tests of verbal fluency, perceptual speed and object location memory (Sanders and Ross-Field, 1986; Gladue *et al.*, 1990; McCormick and Witelson, 1991; Hall and Kimura, 1995; Wegesin, 1998a; Neave *et al.*, 1999; Rahman and Wilson, 2003c; Rahman, Wilson and Abrahams, 2003; Rahman, Abrahams and Wilson, 2003; Rahman, Wilson and Abrahams, 2004a). However, we found no sexual-orientation-related differences in a test of the ability to decode emotions of faces; in fact, we did not find the expected sex difference either (Rahman, Wilson and Abrahams, 2004b).

The cognitive differences between gay and straight people described above could not be accounted for by differences in overall mental ability (i.e. general intelligence or IQ); they remained even after statistical correction for this factor. The characteristic profiles seem to be present in childhood, as gender-nonconforming boys (gender nonconformity being highly pre-dictive of adult homosexuality, as we shall see in Chapter 8) also show diminished spatial ability compared to control boys (Finegan *et al.*, 1982; Grimshaw *et al.*, 1991).

Nick Neave and colleagues (1999) reported that the decrement shown by gay men on mental rotation skills was related to *higher* circulating testosterone (T) levels in this group. This accords with a 'curvilinear' hypothesis concerning the effects of T on spatial ability in men, such that either high or low levels produce decrements in performance (Nyborg, 1994). However, this literature is inconsistent (e.g. Silverman *et al.*, 1999); it is by no means clear that gay men have higher circulating testosterone than straight men, and no study has as yet fully confirmed the curvilinearity hypothesis within straight men. In gay men it is possible that the higher levels of T reflect an 'activational' effect owing to task difficulty or a differing pattern of brain organization *in utero*. In the previous chapters we noted certain paradoxical indications of higher peripheral T in gay men than straight men, and considered possible compensatory ('homeostatic') mechanisms that might account for this (e.g. circulating T working overtime because of the unresponsiveness of certain prenatally set brain-switches).

The data for lesbian women are less consistent than those for gay men. There are trends towards more male-like cognitive performance but these are often non-significant (Wegesin, 1998a). Lesbian women do seem to be more accurate than heterosexual women on targeting tests (a masculine tendency) and they are also more male-like on verbal fluency (Hall and Kimura, 1995; Rahman, Abrahams and Wilson, 2003). Overall, the performance of lesbians is more sex-typical than that of gay men. This suggests that critical periods for the neurodevelopment of sexual preference and sex-dimorphic cognitive ability differ between gay men and lesbian women. For example, it is possible that the prenatal factors which cause cross-sex shifts in sexual preference and cognitive ability work up to a point in lesbian women (thus affecting sexual preference and verbal fluency), after which they are 'protected' from further masculinizing effects, whereas gay men go further down the sex-atypical route of development. (Remember, the term sex-atypical is not meant as a value judgement, just a statistical observation of the observed patterns.) Figure 7.7 summarizes the standardized scores for heterosexual and homosexual performance on certain sex-differentiated cognitive skills from our own research.

Performance on many of these cognitive tests appears to depend on specific brain regions. Mental rotation and spatial perception depend heavily on a region called the parietal lobe, verbal fluency depends on several regions in the frontal portions of the brain (particularly regions called the inferior frontal gyrus and the dorsolateral prefrontal cortex) and temporal lobes if the fluency is for categories of things. Spatial navigation and spatial memory for the locations of objects depend on a structure called the hippocampus. Of course, these areas do not function in isolation (almost certainly they are part of a network of structures involved in the execution of these complex cognitive abilities), but research consistently focuses on the role of these brain regions. The findings of cognitive differences between straight and gay men suggest that the two groups might differ in the structure and/or functioning of parietal regions, some frontal cortical regions (inferior frontal cortex and dorsolateral prefrontal cortex) and the hippocampus. The differences in verbal fluency suggest that straight and lesbian women may differ in some aspects of frontal and temporal lobe functions. Some of the locations for possible gay–straight brain differences are shown in Figure 7.8.

Figure 7.7. Neurocognitive profiles of heterosexual and homosexual men and women. (Reprinted from Rahman, Wilson and Abrahams [2004c] with permission from Elsevier.)

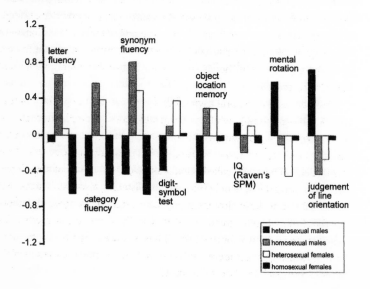

Figure 7.8. Sites for possible gay–straight brain differences based on the cognitive data.

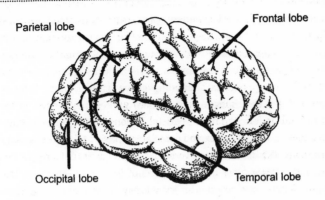

Parietal lobe

Frontal lobe

Occipital lobe

Temporal lobe

Brain asymmetry

The cross-sex shifts in cognitive performance shown by homosexuals might occur because of some other major difference in the way the brain is organized. The best contender is the division of labour between each side of the brain (or hemisphere) in controlling language and spatial abilities. This is variously called functional cerebral asymmetry, hemispheric lateralization or cerebral dominance. It refers primarily to which hemisphere of the brain is dominant for language functions. In most cases it is the left hemisphere – the right hemisphere taking major control of spatial and emotional processes.

We can test for cerebral asymmetry by examining the performance of people on cognitive tasks while in a brain scanner (for example, in functional magnetic resonance imaging; fMRI). Behaviourally, we can examine the extent to which people process visual stimuli presented to either side of the visual field (in what are called visual half-field tests) or verbal stimuli presented to either the right or left ear (dichotic listening tests). More responses to the left side of the environment implicate a right hemisphere preference for that task, whereas greater sensitivity to the right field suggests a left hemisphere preference for that task. This is because the pathways from the primary sense organs (the eyes and ears) cross over to the opposite side of the brain before reaching the cerebral cortex.

Evidence from many different sources, including the effects of damage to various sectors of the brain, indicates that men are more strongly lateralized than women. For example, language processing is almost entirely restricted to the left hemisphere in men, whereas women use the two hemispheres almost equally (in other words, women are 'bilaterally organized' for language). It is possible that this difference may account for the male advantage on spatial tasks because language functions may be displaced from the right hemisphere in favour of spatial processing (Levy and Heller, 1992; Hiscock *et al.*, 1994; 1995). Specialization of the male right brain for spatial ability could also have occurred at the expense of emotional processing, thus accounting for the greater empathy of women and the male preponderance of Asperger's (mind-blindness) tendencies.

Behaviourally speaking, gay men have been found to show reduced language and visual lateralization on dichotic-listening and visual half-field tests when compared to straight men, whereas lesbian women do not differ from straight women (Sanders and Ross-Field, 1986; McCormick and Witelson, 1994; Sanders and Wright, 1997; Wegesin, 1998b). This suggests that gay men are more bilaterally organized for language (like straight women), and are thus perhaps more right-lateralized for spatial ability. Recordings of electrical activity in the brain provide further support for this idea of a female-typical brain asymmetry in gay men. Joel Alexander and Kenneth Sufka from Iowa State University published an initial report in 1993 on the brain activity patterns (using an electroencephalograph or EEG) of nine straight men, ten straight women and five gay men (Alexander and Sufka, 1993). They found that a specific type of brain activity (called alpha) in gay men resembled that of straight women when they were performing a verbal task in which volunteers had to judge which of two words conveyed a happy sentiment, and judgements as to which of two chimeric faces (split vertically so that the two sides show different expressions) was the happier looking. Although interesting, this study was limited by its small sample size and its restriction to one type of brain activity. Furthermore, the type of cognitive task used was not established as showing differences between gay and straight men and women, so we cannot know if the brain activity differences are general or task-specific.

In 1995 Martin Reite and his colleagues from the University of Colorado Health Sciences Centre published a study of the brain activity patterns of eight gay and nine straight men using a different technique, called magnetoencephalography (MEG). The researchers delivered noises to the volunteers through earphones while recording their MEG responses. They were specifically interested in one type of MEG activity, called the M100 component, which is known to be more symmetrical in women than men. Gay men responded in the female-typical fashion compared to straight men. As the M100 originates primarily in a region of the brain called the superior temporal gyrus, it is possible that there are gay–straight differences in this region in men. Nonetheless, this study also suffers from small sample size and there was no direct comparison group of straight women (neither were lesbian women tested – a common omission in this field of inquiry).

A study by Domonick Wegesin, then of the University of Minnesota, addressed some of the problems with the previous research (Wegesin, 1998c). He tested 20 straight men, 20 straight women, 20 gay men and 20 lesbians while they performed mental rotation and verbal tasks known to be sexually dimorphic. He also measured their brain activity using the EEG, time-locked to performance on the tests so as to provide a direct window to the link between brain function and task performance. Wegesin found no differences between heterosexuals and homosexuals in asymmetry of brain processes, but a specific type of EEG pattern (called 'slow wave activity') elicited during the mental rotation task was similar for gay men and straight women. There was also a suggestion of more male-typical slow wave activity in lesbians, but this was not statistically significant.

In summary, the available evidence suggests a bilateral brain organization of language function in gay men that is female-typical. The study by Wegesin seems to confirm a neurophysiological basis for the similarity in mental rotation ability between straight women and gay men but tells us little about brain asymmetry for spatial functions. Nonetheless, based on previous thinking about general sex differences in brain asymmetry (see above), it is reasonable to suspect that a bilateral representation of language in gay men incurs the cost of reduced spatial ability.

Handedness and sexual orientation

Another indirect measure of brain asymmetry is handedness – a person's propensity to use either the right hand or left hand. Greater use of the right hand indicates that language is probably lateralized to the left hemisphere of the brain, and vice versa for left-hand use. This is a contentious area for sex researchers because handedness is an imperfect marker of brain organization (many left-handers still show left-hemisphere dominance for language), plus we do not know about the precise causes of handedness in the first place. Generally, men show more left-handedness than women or, to be more precise, less strict right-handedness (this is called 'non-consistent right-handedness') than do women (Lalumiere *et al.*, 2000). Some researchers have proposed that prenatal androgens are responsible for male 'sinistrality' (another term for non-right-handedness), and that sex differences in language and spatial functions are a consequence (Geschwind and Galaburda, 1985a; 1985b).

A possible prediction from all these considerations is that gay men should show more right-handedness and lesbians should show less. Well, that idea is only half right. A 'meta-analysis' (statistical combination of some 20 available studies) of handedness as related to sexuality found that homosexuals overall (of both sexes) have a 39 per cent greater chance of being non-right-handed. Broken down by sex, gay men had a 34 per cent increase in the odds of being non-right-handed and lesbians had a 91 per cent increase. Results were unaffected by other factors such as the measure of sexual orientation used or HIV status. These findings are consistent with a pattern of greater masculinization in lesbians for several other traits (see Chapter 5). Although inconsistent with the hypothesis above, the results for men can be read as consistent with the fact that gay men show hyper-masculinization in other traits such as finger-length ratios, self-reported genital size and average evoked potentials (see Chapter 5). We return to this issue shortly.

There might be a more direct neuroanatomical basis for these reported differences in markers of brain asymmetry between straight and gay men, involving the tracts of white matter connecting the two halves of the brain, along which information is passed between them. Roger Gorski's doctoral student Laura Allen investigated this issue with respect to sex and sexual orientation. She was interested in a particular tract linking the two hemispheres of the brain called the anterior commissure (AC). In an earlier study by Allen and Gorski (1991), the AC had been reported as larger in women than in men. Then in 1992 Allen and Gorski reported, in a study of 90 postmortem brains from gay men and straight men and women, that the AC was also larger in gay than straight men. However, another report by Mitchell Lasco and his colleagues from New York University of 120 post-mortem brains revealed neither sex nor sexual orientation differences in the size of the AC (Lasco *et al.*, 2002). One study from researchers at McMaster University in Canada, using structural magnetic resonance imaging (MRI), examined the other major white matter tract of the brain – the corpus callosum (CC). They reported that a region of the CC called the 'isthmus' was larger by around 13 per cent in 11 right-handed gay men as compared to ten straight men (Scamvougeras *et al.*, 1994). The isthmus also appears to be larger in women generally, and its size is related to non-right-handedness in men – the larger it is, the more non-right handed men appear to be (Witelson, 1989; Witelson and Goldsmith, 1991).

The finding of a larger isthmus in gay men could connect up the findings on handedness, cognitive ability, and even the higher circulating testosterone levels reported by Nick Neave and his colleagues. A larger isthmus in gay men would allow greater interconnection of right and left language regions. This could underlie the pattern of female-typical language abilities, reduced spatial ability and increased non-right-handedness among gay men. Elevated levels of circulating testosterone have been found to relate to an increased size of the CC (including the isthmus) in men (e.g. Moffat *et al.*, 1997). Testosterone may act to promote white matter growth – there is evidence that white matter is rich in some of the enzymes that help metabolize testosterone to its more powerful agents such as DHT (Celotti *et al.*, 1992). Thus the larger isthmus in gay men might be a result of greater prenatal T exposure, as implicated by the somatic evidence detailed in Chapter 5. Left-handed men (these research studies did not ask about sexual orientation) have significantly larger isthmuses than do right-handed men, and less language lateralization (Witelson, 1989; Habib *et al.*, 1991; Cowell *et al.*, 1993). As a consequence of these asymmetries, spatial ability might be compromised, hence the association between T levels and poorer performance on mental rotations among gay men (Neave *et al.*, 1999).

It is possible that the greater development of white matter tissue (in the CC) stimulated by the excess testosterone (specifically its metabolite, DHT) in gay men during foetal development permits the right hemisphere to become mostly dominant, thus shifting handedness and the lateralization of language towards a bilateral representation within the brain. This would account for the elevated rate of non-right-handedness in men generally, and gay men and lesbian women (for whom the 'masculinization' pathway is more linear) particularly. Martin Lalumiere and colleagues (2000) have argued that a prenatal androgen explanation cannot be the whole picture because it explains the association between non-right-handedness and homosexuality in women but not in men, if one follows the standard prediction from the theory (see above). However, here we have shown that thinking about the mechanisms for prenatal hormonal action in *specific* or 'localized' terms, as Dennis McFadden would put it, could account for non-right-handedness in gay men. Clearly, such an idea is speculative at present. Further evidence bearing upon it from the fields of neuroimaging, neuropsychology and neuroendocrinology is awaited.

Conclusion

Many of the research findings outlined above will appear confusing to the lay reader. In that case it may be reassuring that the scientists responsible for them are almost equally confused, for indeed the facts are complex and we are far from any firm conclusions. What does seem clear, however, is that neurological differences between straight men and women do exist, and that sexual orientation differences also connect with brain structure and functions. Deep, instinctive parts of the brain, such as the hypothalamus and limbic system, certainly seem to be involved, but so too are 'higher' centres, and the way in which the left and right sides of the brain are differentiated.

In many instances, gay men are found to be more like women and lesbians show some similarities to men (cross-sex shifts). Equally interesting is the finding that in certain other respects gay men and lesbians are typical of their own sex. Any satisfactory theory of the origins of homosexuality in men and women will have to take account of these complex patterns, and it becomes increasingly clear that we need to focus on the impact of genes and hormones on brain development rather than variations in social experiences and upbringing.

CHAPTER EIGHT

Childhood indications

ITTLE BOYS NOTORIOUSLY like to play with guns and tractors, while girls prefer dolls and cuddly toys. Parents who try to reverse or neutralize this pattern have an uphill struggle. Given a tractor, a little girl is likely to cuddle and nurture it, calling it a 'dear little tractor'; given a doll, a boy is just as likely to test the limits of its mechanical endurance by pulling the limbs off it. Alternatively, if the boy and girl are siblings, they will probably just arrange an amicable exchange of toys. But what does it mean when a child spontaneously chooses to play with toys that are traditionally associated with the opposite sex? Adults and peers are likely to tease them and call them names, such as 'sissy' or 'tomboy'. But does it mean that they are on track to become gay?

In this chapter we consider evidence concerning the extent to which a gay, lesbian or straight adulthood can be predicted on the basis of observations of childhood behaviour, such as sex-typical or sex-atypical toy preferences, play style or preferred playmates. Certainly, it is widely believed that feminine boys become gay men and masculine or tomboyish girls become lesbians. Children who act in a sex-typical manner, on the other hand, are expected to grow up heterosexual. To some, these ideas might seem like ill-considered stereotypes, but research shows that there is definitely some truth in them. There is also some interesting research showing that gay men and lesbians have early recollections of feeling 'different' from other children.

Feminine boys and masculine girls

One of the strongest findings in the area of sexual orientation research is that children who become gay or lesbian ('pre-gay' children) adhere less strictly to gender norms than children who become heterosexual adults – that is, gay men and lesbians show greater childhood gender nonconformity

(CGN) than heterosexuals of both sexes. Studies have used two key methods: one approach asks gays, lesbians and heterosexuals to recall or check specific types of childhood sex-typed behaviours. An example of a question could be to rate one's agreement (say on a scale ranging from one for *strongly disagree* to seven for *strongly agree*) with the statement '*As a child, I disliked competitive sports such as football, baseball and basketball.*' This would be a retrospective study. The other type of study is a prospective one, which follows up young feminine boys, masculine girls and control children into adulthood to examine their ultimate sexual orientation.

There have been plenty of objective retrospective studies – far too many to detail here. Fortunately, Mike Bailey and Ken Zucker have done us the favour of reviewing over 40 such retrospective studies to examine the overall link between CGN and adult sexual orientation (Bailey and Zucker, 1995). Compared to heterosexual men, gay men (as children) were found to have engaged in less rough-and-tumble play, less aggressive behaviour, less competitive athletic sports, were less involved in boy-typical toys and games, preferred girls as playmates, cross-dressed more, had less male-typical career aspirations and had reputations for being sissies. Compared to heterosexual women, lesbians tended as children to be more physically active (engage in more rough-and-tumble play, sports, etc.), had more boys as playmates, wore male-typical clothes and were likely to have reputations as tomboys.

The degree of these differences (called 'effect size' by statisticians) is large between straight and gay men (about 1.3 standard deviations) and only slightly less so between straight and lesbian women (about 1.0). Putting this into a more easily understood context, Bailey and Zucker estimated that an average gay man is more feminine on the childhood sex-typed measures than around 90 per cent of heterosexual men. Interestingly, gay men also appeared to be more variable in their memories than heterosexual men. That is, heterosexual men tend to bunch more at the lower end of the scales (such as the one mentioned above), indicating a strong denial of any femininity during their childhoods. Gay men have a greater range in their responses, around 20 per cent showing similar scores to straight men and many others with extremely feminine scores. It is unlikely that gay men are intentionally recalling more feminine behaviour as there is some tendency among gay men to be as 'femiphobic' as straight men, showing discomfort with the idea of childhood femininity (and, indeed, adult femininity). In any case, as we shall see, prospective work definitively supports the link between CGN and adult sexual orientation. Perhaps, then, there is genuine variation among gay men, raising the question of whether gay men who were feminine as children differ in some way from those who were masculine boys. We will revisit the notion of variation among gays and lesbians in the next chapter.

At least in the case of males, prospective studies provide strong support to the retrospective work. Unfortunately, there are no prospective studies in females although work is under way to examine this (Bailey *et al.*, 2002). The most famous study is by Richard Green, then at UCLA (now retired as director of the Gender Identity Clinic at Charing Cross Hospital). He began his study in the late 1960s, recruiting 66 boys (aged four to ten years) who exhibited markedly feminine behaviour. Around 70 per cent of these boys engaged in cross-dressing, over 50 per cent played with dolls, 60 per cent engaged in girl-typical play, over 80 per cent stated an occasional wish to be a girl and almost 80 per cent disliked rough-and-tumble play and sports participation. Such tendencies were virtually absent among a control group of 56 masculine boys. Parents reported that some of these feminine behaviours appeared as early as three years. Green interviewed the boys and their parents repeatedly during childhood, adolescence and early adulthood as far as he could (by final follow-up, at average age of 19, he collected data from around two thirds of initial group of boys).

The key finding of Green's study is striking. Around 75 per cent of the young men who had been feminine boys reported sexual attraction to men, compared with only one young man who had been a typically masculine boy. All the other typically masculine boys appeared to be completely heterosexual (Green, 1987). As some of these boys had their final interviews in their mid-teens (the youngest was 14), it is possible that more of the feminine boys would ultimately turn out homosexual, thus raising the figure higher than 75 per cent. Some of the 25 per cent who denied attraction to men at final interview could have been 'closeted' or as yet unsure of their true orientation. Green writes of some men who denied homosexuality only later to admit a lack of honesty. One of the feminine boys also expressed an interest in becoming a woman. Although Green expected that very feminine boys would become transsexual, this only happened to one of the boys. The association between CGN and adult homosexuality is thus pretty well established in men.

CGN, learning and prenatal factors

Such an association between childhood traits and adult sexual orientation certainly weakens social learning theories that put down homosexuality to 'incestuous' experiences during childhood or puberty, and other 'acquisition' models. The data suggest that the behavioural antecedents to adult sexual orientation can be observed early on. These in turn are most likely laid down by genetic and other prenatal factors. As mentioned in Chapter 1, Bailey and colleagues in the Australian twin study found that CGN was more heritable than sexual orientation *per se*, indicating a strong genetic basis. This does not necessarily mean that sexual orientation is any less genetic, but it does suggest that CGN is 'closer' to the genes. Perhaps it mops up more of the statistical variance between individuals that can be traced back to genetic factors because it is a more continuous variable. The relationship between CGN and adult homosexuality appears to hold for men and women across several different cultures, confirming its stability and universality (Whitam and Zent, 1984; Whitam and Mathy, 1991).

The studies on various intersex conditions (Chapter 5) provide perhaps the strongest evidence that the development of gender-related traits (including those that are antecedents to adult homosexuality) is determined early on by prenatal hormones. In many of the cases of mistakenly sex-reassigned children, the individual was gender nonconforming in certain ways (in line with their genetic sex), such as being dominant within their peer groups or in play style. Girls exposed to high levels of prenatal androgens because of CAH (who, remember, also show higher rates of same-sex attraction) show more masculine childhood play behaviours than control females. This has been found in studies interviewing both the girls and their mothers, retrospective interviews with adults and direct observations of play style and toy preferences. The behaviours most influenced are rough-and-tumble play, preference for boys as playmates, increased interest in cars and trucks and reduced interest in dolls (Berenbaum and Hines, 1992; Berenbaum and Snyder, 1995; Zucker *et al.*, 1996). CAH studies may actually underestimate the effects because it is likely that, although these girls want to engage in boy-typical play, boys may not want them to take part, preferring instead to play fight with other boys. Women with androgen insensitivity also usually report female-typical childhood toy, activities and playmate preferences (Hines *et al.*, 2003), despite one historically famous case – that of Joan of Arc (whose medical records revealed lack of menstruation and pubic hair, suggesting that she might have been genetically male).

The role of prenatal sex hormones is thus well established. Maternal stress, however, seems to be of minimal importance. As already noted (Chapter 5), a prospective study by Hines *et al.* (2002) found that prenatal stress had no influence on childhood gender role behaviours in boys and negligible effects in girls.

In animals there is evidence that testosterone plays a major role in mediating aspects of juvenile sex-typed behaviour, such as play fighting (the animal equivalent of rough-and-tumble play). Castrating male rats reduces play fighting to female-typical levels, whereas prenatal testosterone treatment can make female rats play fight at male-typical levels (Pellis, 2002). A region of the brain called the amygdala might be the site of the action of androgens in controlling juvenile play fighting (Meany and McEwen, 1986). As this structure is also sexually dimorphic, it might have some role to play in juvenile sex-typical behaviours and sexual orientation in humans. Recall also (Chapter 6) that feminine boys typically have more older brothers than typically masculine boys, and feminine boys with two or more older brothers have lower birth weights than feminine and control boys with fewer than two older brothers (Blanchard *et al.*, 2002). Thus the maternal immunity hypothesis may also explain the link between childhood femininity and adult homosexuality in men.

The brains of children who show strong CGN may also differ from those of other children in a manner similar to those of adult gay men. One Canadian study by Joanne Finegan and colleagues recruited 13 feminine boys (classed as having gender identity disorder), eight control brothers and ten boys referred for other psychiatric assessments (a good extra control measure to see if psychiatric referral in general was associated with psychological differences). All boys were administered a standard ability test battery, the Wechsler Intelligence Scale (there are separate versions for children and adults), which includes verbal and spatial tests. The three groups of boys did not differ in overall intellectual ability (their IQs), but the feminine boys were substantially poorer on a spatial test called Block Design, one on which males characteristically outperform females (Finegan *et al.*, 1982). In another Canadian study 101 feminine boys (diagnosed with gender identity disorder) demonstrated significantly higher verbal than spatial scores. A second sample of 33 feminine boys showed lower spatial skills than 'psychiatric control' boys, while a third final sample of 24 feminine boys showed lower spatial scores than 24 normal control boys (Grimshaw *et al.*, 1991). These findings are consistent with those discussed in Chapter 7 showing that adult gay men have lower spatial ability than straight men (i.e. are cross-sex shifted so as to be more like females in this mode of cognitive functioning). In Chapter 7 we also discussed how specific brain regions control certain cognitive skills, such as the parietal lobes in some types of spatial ability. Thus there appears to be a common neural basis for the childhood antecedents of adult homosexuality.

Adult 'psychological gender'

It is perhaps not surprising to find that masculine childhood interests continue on to masculine adult interests and feminine childhood interests to feminine adult interests. This also means that the adult interests of gay men and lesbians might be part of their broader gender nonconformity during childhood. We are all familiar with the stereotypes about gay men, lesbians and straight people and their interests. Gay men are seen to enjoy female-typical activities like shopping, fashion, style, dancing, acting and singing and prefer people-related professions. This view is typified in the joke about the 'gay mafia' – 'If you don't pay the protection, they send round a couple of the boys to criticize your wallpaper.' By contrast, heterosexual men are into sport, cars, mechanics and hands-on or competitive types of occupations. The stereotypes for lesbians versus straight women are equally well known. The point is that, contrary to political correctness, many of these stereotypes are accurate, at least when we talk about them in terms of averages. Obviously, not all gay men are like straight women and not all lesbians are like straight men, but there are some interesting and large psychological differences that cannot be ignored.

Richard Lippa has conducted much research on differences in 'psychological gender' between people of different sexual orientations. He devised a questionnaire based on around 100 occupational and recreational interests (assessing degree of interest in fashion, being a nurse, designer, engineer, etc). Large samples of men and women, gay and straight, rated these items, and Lippa has consistently found large sex differences between heterosexual men and women (an effect size of around 2.0), even in university samples, where the majority are headed towards professional occupations of one sort or another and one might expect more liberation from traditional sex-role stereotypes. Gay men's scores are found to be in between those of heterosexual men and women, although more towards the female-typical end, and the scores of lesbians are more towards the male-typical end. The effect sizes are still large, if less than those of the heterosexual sex differences (Lippa, 2000; 2002). Lippa has also found that the gay–straight differences are larger in people from cultures with strong traditions of strict differentiation between male and female gender roles, compared to those from Western cultures where there is a movement towards less gender polarization. Nevertheless, the same gay–straight differences were apparent across various cultures (Lippa and Tan, 2001). Lippa has also discovered a strong genetic component to psychological gender in a study of twins (Lippa and Hershberger, 1999). All these data indicate that the gay–straight differences represent real psychological differences that cannot be dismissed as simply cultural; rather they appear to be innate and apparent from early childhood in the form of gender nonconformity.

CGN and psychological health

Are there any health implications of gender-nonconforming behaviour during childhood? Some evidence suggests there might be, not because CGN is pathological in of itself, but rather because of others' reactions to it or how it sets up psychological dispositions which may predispose some adult gay men to certain mental health problems. A pre-gay child's position on the CGN continuum – some outrageously nonconforming, others more conventional – may affect their growing up process. In a sense, strongly nonconformist children 'out' themselves very early on. Parents may already suspect that their child might turn out gay and do everything in their power to prevent it, including inflicting punishment. A 'sissy boy' may quickly become unpopular in the family and particularly in the eyes of the father. Large-scale surveys find that both gay men and lesbians report more physical abuse during their childhoods by their mothers and fathers than do heterosexual men and women (Corliss *et al.*, 2002). These data also suggest that tomboyish behaviour among girls may not be as well tolerated by parents as previously thought. Heather Corliss and colleagues at UCLA think that, because gay men and lesbians display CGN, this places them at risk for maltreatment at the hands of their parents.

The psychoanalytic idea that homosexuality results from a 'smothering', over-protective mother combined with a 'distant' father makes much more sense if we reverse the theoretical cause and effect. Observation of CGN behaviours in a child may lead to hostility and withdrawal on the part of the father (who is disappointed, for example, that his son is not turning out 'red-blooded') as well as compensatory over-protectiveness on the part of the mother.

CGN also predisposes towards engaging in receptive anal intercourse (a sexual risk behaviour for HIV and other sexually transmitted infections) and greater body dissatisfaction among gay men (Weinrich *et al.*, 1992; Strong *et al.*, 2000). Clearly, mental health professionals should be aware of these variations within gay men and lesbians in order to provide competent services.

As we have noted, a pre-gay boy is likely to be less interested in competitive sports than other boys, whereas a pre-lesbian girl may be more interested in these. During the adolescent years gender roles become much stricter, both within peer groups and with respect to the expectations of adults. This may be more of a problem for gender-nonconforming boys than for girls, since some degree of masculinity in a girl may be an advantage. The gender-nonconforming boys may find themselves excluded from both their male and female peer groups, and the feeling of isolation may be compounded by derisive taunts and bullying.

Some may argue that, given all these apparently negative consequences, why not attempt treatment of boys and girls with CGN so as to make them conform more to their assigned traditional sex role? The evidence suggests that treating pre-gay boys (there are no data for pre-lesbian girls) does not alleviate these problems for the simple reason that it does not work. Richard Green's own figures show that nine out of 12 gender-nonconforming boys who were treated with behaviour modification techniques became homosexual adults, no different from what was observed in boys not treated. Rather the degree to which pre-gay children experience psychological problems before and during adolescence varies according to how gender nonconforming they are (which we believe is determined by genetics and prenatal factors), as well as the attitudes of parents, the schools they attend and the community in which they live.

Of course, the strong connection between CGN and adult homosexuality does not mean that we can predict a child's eventual sexual orientation with pinpoint accuracy. This is especially true in the case of women; just because a girl is a tomboy does not mean she is bound to become a lesbian – she may very well turn out straight. On the hand, it is rather fashionable among some scientists (probably because of various politically correct sensibilities) to detail copious amounts of research for a link between two variables and then to back off by saying, 'Well, it's not strong enough to predict anything from.' In the case of males, both the prospective and retrospective work shows that we can make very educated guesses about the eventual sexual orientation of feminine boys. Since it seems improbable that any form of treatment will alter this outcome, we can only hope that parents and society will change towards greater acceptance of minority sexual orientations.

CHAPTER NINE

Are there different types?

AS WE HAVE seen in Chapter 8, there appears to be some psychological variation *within* the gay and lesbian population. Terms such as 'butch' and 'femme' and 'top' and 'bottom' have typically been used to categorize homosexuals of both sexes in terms of specific gender roles or sexual behaviours. To what extent are these meaningful differences? Currently the science on this question is very thin, but there is some suggestion that within-sexual-orientation variation could arise from biological factors.

Perceptions

The stereotype that there are two types of gay men and two types of lesbian women is often found in the vocabulary of gay men and lesbians themselves. Regarding lesbians, the two types are commonly referred to as 'butch' and 'femme', although more colourful epithets like 'diesel dyke' and 'lipstick lesbian' have also been applied. A butch lesbian is one who is masculine in terms of dress, physical appearance and behaviour, and is also dominant (adopting the male role) in sexual activity. A femme lesbian is more feminine in appearance and interests, and is usually the passive partner in sex. Among gay men, the two types are sometimes called 'top' and 'bottom' and primarily refer to the sexual position taken – a top takes the active, insertive role and bottom the receptive role. However, tops may also be more generally masculine and bottoms more feminine overall. Many dispute the validity of this typology, seeing it as an attempt to fit homosexuals into a heterosexual relationship style that mimics the heterosexual pattern of a masculine partner with a feminine partner.

There is a great deal of debate around this and much historical and sociological literature, but as this is a book about the science of sexual orientation we will not get bogged down in these issues here. Suffice it to say that from the early twentieth century until now such typologies have several times gone in and out of fashion, both among gay men and lesbians, and heterosexual academics alike. In the early 1950s these categories were widely accepted, but a decade later (when feminists in particular were generally opposed to classification and biological theories about sexuality) they tended to be rejected as patriarchal and anti-gay. More recently there has been a move towards acceptance of them again (the 1980s saw a resurgence, particularly among lesbians, in adopting butch and femme distinctions as valid expressions of sexual diversity). It is particularly interesting that it is homosexual people themselves who have reasserted the use of butch–femme terms and other typologies. Many gay men and lesbians would find odd the protestations of the mostly heterosexual feminists (and other postmodernists) about how gay people should express themselves sexually.

Despite the resurgence in recognition of these typologies in the twenty-first century, they remain subject to change and confusion (confusion especially for researchers!). Lesbians in particular are less likely to adhere to the strict types postulated in previous times. For example, the current terms 'lipstick lesbian' and 'baby dyke' often to refer to 'types' that are ambiguous with respect to their self-presentation, showing mixed signals and complex patterns of masculine and feminine roles and preferences. Among gay men, the terms 'top' and 'bottom' do not necessarily hold up in survey studies of gay men's actual sexual behaviour. On the other hand, studies examining the personal advertisements of gay men show that the majority describe their preferred sexual role as bottom and seek tops as partners (Bailey *et al.*, 1997).

The research

Regarding the scientific research, we should consider the possibility that the studies we will discuss below may be recruiting (perhaps through ascertainment biases, as discussed in Chapter 3) certain biologically stricter subtypes. This would not invalidate the research but rather highlight the fact that there are much smaller subtypes within a generally more 'gender-bending' gay and lesbian population. Perhaps also the words used, such as butch and femme, are considered dated, or even offensive, so many gay men and lesbians might not want to identify with them. If we could find other, more acceptable terms, perhaps more subjects would be prepared to classify themselves. In other words, the psychological subtypes might be real, even though there is dispute or sensitivity with respect to the labels that are applied which could affect the self-report and volunteer rates.

The fact that around 30 per cent of gay men (and perhaps more for lesbians) were not gender-nonconforming as children (that is, they report sex-typical behaviour) suggests some variability. It would be surprising if these childhood differences were not to some extent innate and ultimately did not translate into adult behaviour. Therefore there might be some validity to these individual differences. Also, uncommonly for sexual orientation research, almost all the current studies on homosexual subtypes have been conducted on women.

Early work (Bell *et al.*, 1981) suggested that two types of lesbians might be identified on the basis of the extent of childhood gender nonconformity (CGN). These researchers found groups of masculine lesbians and non-masculine lesbians (including a subset of who rated themselves as 'highly feminine'). Masculine lesbians reported greater CGN than non-masculine lesbians but, importantly, a statistical analysis showed that there seemed to be a direct (causative?) path from recalled CGN to masculine lesbianism. For the non-masculine lesbians, homosexual experiences during adolescence seemed to be important for adult lesbianism. Now although this could be taken to suggest that inborn factors play more of a role in some types of female homosexuality (i.e. in masculine lesbianism) than others (non-masculine lesbianism), it is too early say this with certainty. It is possible that inborn factors determine female homosexuality overall, and that other (environmental) factors determine the subtyping. Among gay men, we have already noted (Chapter 8) that gay men who prefer the receptive role during sex were more likely than other gay men to recall greater CGN (Weinrich *et al.*, 1992).

A study by Loulan (1990), which examined self-reports of lesbians for the butch–femme distinction, provided interesting clues about possible physical differences. Volunteers from all over the US were asked to rate themselves on a nine-point scale from 'ultimate femme' to 'ultimate butch'. Most lesbians (around 44 per cent) rated themselves in the middle of the scale (we might call these 'androgynous', although this term is problematic). However, 25 per cent rated themselves as femme, and 19 per cent as butch. Interestingly, 36 per cent of the butch lesbians said that they were mistaken for a man, compared to 4 per cent of femmes (and 25 per cent of androgynous lesbians). Seventy-nine per cent of femmes said they passed as straight compared to 23 per cent of butches (and 42 per cent of androgynous lesbians). Clearly, something in the physical appearance of these subtypes appears to be cross-sex shifted – butches in the male direction and femmes in the female-typical direction. Of course, this could be partly down to self-presentation, that is the way butch lesbians may wear male-typical clothing, crop their hair and even change the way they talk and walk, but that begs the question of why this subtype of lesbian 'chooses' to present themselves in masculine mode in the first place. The motivations responsible for this choice are themselves likely to have their origins in inborn factors.

In fact, research that examines physical appearance more objectively supports the notion of true physical differences between subtypes. Perkins (1981) interviewed 241 lesbians for two to three hours each and classified them into 'dominant' (male-like), 'passive' (female-like) and 'intermediate' on the basis of those performing male-like or female-like sexual acts. Weight, height and several body measurements were also taken, and Perkins found that dominant lesbians, contrasted with passive and intermediate types, were taller, had broader shoulder width, narrower hips, and greater arm and leg thickness.

Sex hormone comparisons

Is there any evidence that subtypes of lesbians are differentiated in terms of hormone levels? Unfortunately the evidence is conflicting in this area, with respect to both prenatal and adult hormone levels. Sharon Pearcey and her colleagues from Georgia State University in Atlanta asked individuals in 28 lesbian couples to rate themselves and their partners as butch or femme on a nine-point scale, and took testosterone (T) measurements from saliva samples. Individuals with higher butch ratings had higher T levels than their partners, but this effect only appeared within couples and did not hold for unrelated groups of women (Pearcey *et al.*, 1996). The participants' self-rating of butch or femme conformed to how their partners rated them, thus showing that the terms have shared meanings, at least within couples.

Another study, by Christine Dancey from Goldsmiths College in London, examined 40 lesbians who were classified into 'primary' lesbians (masculine lesbians who had no heterosexual experience) and 'secondary' lesbians (those with previous heterosexual experience). There were also control groups of heterosexual women and intermediate lesbians. This study examined several hormones from blood samples (testosterone, oestrogen, progesterone and androstenedione) and also controlled for menstrual cycle phase. Dancey reported no differences in hormone levels between the groups and suggested that the distinction between primary and secondary lesbians is invalid (Dancey, 1990).

The major study in this area is by Devendra Singh and colleagues at the University of Texas, Austin (Singh *et al.*, 1999). Their work followed the standard prenatal androgen theory model for sexual orientation, and they argued that variations in androgens during critical periods of female sexual development produce subtypes in erotic identification in lesbians. They examined 100 lesbians and 58 heterosexual women. Lesbian women were asked to respond to two statements, one asking whether they thought of themselves primarily as butch and the other whether they viewed themselves as primarily femme. Responses were on a ten-point scale from 'definitely not true' to 'definitely true'. The women were classed as butch if they rated themselves higher on the butch than the femme scale, and vice versa for femme. There was a strong negative association between responses on the butch scale and responses on the femme scale, confirming that they were indeed measuring opposite ends of the same underlying dimension. There were 47 butch lesbians and 53 femme lesbians. All women were examined on traits which are known to differentiate between men and women and which probably reflect prenatal sex hormones, such as the waist-to-hip ratio (women have lower waist-to-hip ratios than men because of the prenatal androgens affecting the distribution of body fat). CGN and psychological dispositions, such as the desire to give birth and raise children, body image satisfaction, symptoms of depression, sexual practices and sexually dimorphic personality traits such as expressiveness and competitiveness were also recorded, as well as saliva testosterone levels. Butch and femme lesbians were found not to differ either from each other or from heterosexual women on sex-linked personality traits, depression scores or body satisfaction levels. However, butch lesbians recalled more CGN, had higher waist-to-hip ratios, higher salivary T levels and less desire to give birth than both femme lesbians and heterosexual women. Compared to femmes, butch lesbians took the 'top' sexual position more often and had more sexual relationships over the preceding two years. Femme lesbians recalled more CGN than heterosexual women, but were also more willing to raise children than them. Thus in some respects butch lesbians were more male-typical than femmes. However, lesbians of both kinds were more male-typical than heterosexual women in CGN, as might be expected given the robust association of this measure with adult homosexuality.

Finger-length ratios

In Singh's study we see that (apart from circulating T) one marker of pre-natal sex hormone influences, waist-to-hip ratio, was masculinized in butch lesbians, indicating exposure to higher levels of androgens *in utero*. Are there any other indicators? Windy Brown and her colleagues (from Marc Breedlove's lab) examined differences in finger-length ratios (2D:4D; see Chapter 5) between self-identified butch and femme lesbians. The researchers recruited men and women from a Gay Pride event held in Oakland, California. Volunteers were asked about their sexual orientation and had photocopies of their hands taken using a portable photocopier. They were also asked to check 'butch' or 'femme' if they had to describe themselves as one of these two types. They recruited 267 women and 168 men, and found the usual sex difference in 2D:4D. Of the 267 women, 29 were heterosexual, 28 claimed to be bisexual and 207 of the women were les-bians. Among the lesbians, 87 identified themselves as butch, 89 as femme and 31 did not answer the question. The 2D:4D ratios of butch lesbians were lower (i.e. more masculinized) than those of femme lesbians. This difference was only apparent on the right hand, and even this barely reached statistical significance (Brown *et al.*, 2002). In other words, the difference is small and there was considerable overlap in 2D:4D ratios between the self-identified groups of lesbian women. Also, since the study did not report comparisons with heterosexual women, or findings for the male group, it must be pre-sumed that no significant differences were found.

Another small study by a researcher at Rutgers University reported lower 2D:4D in butch lesbians compared to femme lesbians and heterosexual controls but her sample was only 25 lesbians and 23 heterosexual women (Tortorice, 2001). Tortorice did not provide details of the breakdown for the lesbian groups but presumably the numbers would be small.

In our own study of 240 volunteers we also used Singh *et al.*'s method to examine subtypes within both lesbians and gay men. We found a strong negative correlation between the two scales (meaning that higher scores on the butch scale were strongly linked to low scores on the femme scale), as did Singh and his colleagues. Subjects were assigned to the butch group if they rated themselves higher on the butch than the femme scale, or assigned to the femme group if they rated themselves higher on the femme than the butch scale, or 'non-classified' if they scored exactly the same on both items. Among gay men 32 were classed as butch, 15 as femme and 13 as non-classified. Among lesbians, 23 were classed as butch, 26 femme and 11 non-classified. We found that degree of 'butchness' (subtracting femme rating from butch rating for each participant) was completely unrelated to 2D:4D differences between sexual orientation groups. Nor was it associated with the cognitive differences between them (Rahman and Wilson, 2003b; Rahman *et al.*, 2004c). Our data, then, suggest that within-sexual-orientation differences in erotic role identification do not reliably map onto the overall between-group differences in prenatal hormone markers or neurocognitive skills.

Conclusions

The inconsistencies across all these studies do not inspire much confidence in making firm conclusions about what causes subtypes within sexual orientation. The inconsistencies may arise in part from the differing measures used for subtyping (e.g. a 'primary' lesbian may not necessarily be the same as a 'butch' lesbian). The key may be to clarify exactly what terms encapsulate different 'types' for gay men and lesbians in different populations and cultures.

Our brief review of the work above has no doubt excluded multiple other 'subtypes' of gay men and lesbians. For example, there are drag queens, drag kings, and the various gay male sexual subcultures (that is, different from the conventional preference for the prototypical male look) such as leather, S & M (sadomasochistic), bears (preference for hairy men with beer guts) and so on. The research highlighted throughout this book could be relevant to these expressions. Perhaps drag queens are slightly further down the sex-atypical route of neurodevelopment than conventional gay men, but not enough to become full-blown transsexuals. Perhaps these 'types' are further differentiated in childhood sex-typed behaviour, finger-length ratios or other markers of prenatal factors, brain function and even psychosocial factors. The apparent sexual subcultures among gay men, which are not apparent among lesbians, may arise from these factors interacting with brain 'modules' that control the greater male emphasis on sex. All these remain interesting lines for further scientific inquiry, and no doubt future work will shed much light on the inborn and external factors that produce this sexual kaleidoscope.

CHAPTER TEN

The science of sexual orientation and society

IN THE PRECEDING chapters we have detailed the wealth of scientific information showing that sexual orientation is something we are born with and is not 'acquired' from our social environment. It may be useful to recap this evidence as follows:

▶ Sexual orientation is stable and bimodal. If bisexuality exists it is rare, especially in males.

▶ The popular idea that sexual orientation can be influenced by social factors, such as upbringing, contagion or seduction, has no scientific backing.

▶ Genes do influence sexual orientation but contribute less than half of the variance. Their location is still uncertain but they are likely to be genes that affect brain responses to hormones or the enzymes that mediate them.

▶ The survival of gay genes over many millennia suggests that they may have some positive value, reduction of aggression and promotion of same-sex alliances, for example. More likely, they may survive through a balanced polymorphism mechanism.

▶ Evidence from intersex conditions such as congenital adrenal hyperplasia (CAH), finger-length ratios, auditory mechanisms and growth patterns implicates prenatal sex hormones in the developmental origins of sexual orientation.

▶ A fraternal birth order effect in males (gay men having more older brothers) is further support for the role of prenatal hormone or hormone-independent mechanisms (presumably mediated by maternal antibodies that can cross the placenta).

▶ The brains of gay men and lesbian women seem to be cross-sex shifted in certain respects, so more like those of heterosexual women and men respectively.

▶ Sexual orientation can be predicted early in life on the basis of the observation of play patterns and toy preferences.

▶ The existence of subtypes of homosexuals that can be differentiated by hormone patterns is doubtful.

Although we are not ethicists, and it is not our primary purpose to draw moral or social conclusions from our findings, it is virtually impossible not to address these issues briefly. Since the early days of research linking biological factors to behaviour or to psychology, people have expected there to be particular types of moral, legal and political implications. In these concluding comments we therefore offer our own thoughts about what the scientific facts about sexual orientation might mean for people (gay, lesbian or straight) and show that it is not as simple as the reaction it provokes in many.

When the early findings of biological concomitants of sexual orientation (the key ones being Simon LeVay's finding of INAH-3 differences and Dean Hamer's Xq28 finding) appeared there was a furore of public interest and a great deal of concern about what they meant for society. The main issues appeared to centre around whether demonstrating biological correlates to homosexuality (this is how the debate was framed; few considered that the findings were also correlates of heterosexuality!) meant that homosexuals should be shown more acceptance and that oppressive social policies against gay people should be reviewed, or whether they meant that homosexuality was a 'biological disease' that could be 'cured' by medical interventions. In reality there was, and is, much more variability in views about what the biology of sexual orientation might mean. Some scientists and non-scientists in the pro-gay camp use biological explanations to defend homosexuality, while others in the anti-gay camp question the biological evidence and argue for social factors in the acquisition of homosexuality. However, there are plenty of others in the pro-gay camp who also argue for social factors and freedom of choice, as well anti-gays who argue that biology supports a disease model of homosexuality.

We believe we have shown that social factors play no appreciable role in the development of sexual orientation, thus excluding the 'social acquisitionists' from further debate – whether they are pro- or anti-gay. Equally, we have found no evidence that homosexuality is a biological 'disease' or 'error'. For example, there is no evidence supporting the 'developmental instability' hypothesis (see Chapter 5). Nor does being gay ruin people's lives as compe-tent, productive human beings in the way that heart disease, schizophrenia or alcoholism (which have biological precursors) do. Surely this leaves us with the pro-gay view about the biological correlates of homosexuality? Interestingly, surveys also show that people who believe that homosexuality is 'biological' have more positive attitudes towards it than those who believe it to be 'acquired'.

Aaron Greenberg, a lawyer in Chicago, and Mike Bailey (of Northwestern University) have examined these issues in some depth (Greenberg and Bailey, 1993). They argue that the finding of a mere brain difference between heterosexuals and homosexuals (taking LeVay's study here) does not have immediate moral and legal implications: one finds a brain difference – so what? It's just a difference in structure. The error in logic in many people's minds presumably comes from the commonly held view that some behaviour is *not* represented by a brain difference or brain correlate of some kind. But this is clearly false – all behaviour is biologically 'caused' in the sense that it takes place within and is generated by the physical activity of our brains; the chemical and electrical activity that we experience as thoughts and feelings is transmitted to the muscles that move us and glands that affect us. Also, argue Greenberg and Bailey, anything that causes a type of behaviour (e.g. a sexual preference), whether it be environmental, genetic or prenatal, must cause that behaviour by producing a change in the state of the brain. In this sense, every behavioural difference between people must be caused by a brain difference. If all behaviour is biologically based, it makes no logical sense to argue for particular types of moral, political or other consequences for a small subset of these biologically based behaviours, such as homosexuality.

Nonetheless, we would argue that if homosexuality is inborn or innate (as we have shown) then certain social policy consequences might reason-ably follow. At present, many public attitudes and legal policies seem to be founded on the assumption that homosexuality is an acquired or learned phenomenon. For example, it is common to blame parents for making their children gay by faulty or inadequate upbringing. The research we have reviewed has clearly shown this to be false.

Similarly, it would be naïve to say that research which shows that the mental health and sexual orientation of children of gay and lesbian parents is no different to that of the general population has no implications for adoption or parental rights of gay men and lesbians. It clearly does, and they are obvious so we will not spell them out. The fact the sexual orientation cannot be learned should lessen the fears that underlie legislation such as that dictating that educational establishments must not 'promote homosexuality' (the controversial Clause 28 in the UK). Although such laws may act as deterrents to public displays of homosexual behaviour (and they probably have worked to some extent in the past), they do not diminish the underlying innateness of homosexuality or stop individuals acting in accordance with their inborn feelings. It does not appear to make any sense to deter people from acting on innate dispositions that harm no one else and are not contagious to others. It seems to us improper to use theories based on seduction, or other such dated psychosocial theories, for moral or social policy decisions about adult sexual orientation. Such arcane laws may also have knock-on effects, causing other problems, such as poorer safe-sex education and mental health services for young gay men and lesbians.

The particular sexual attractions and desires of homosexual people may constitute durable traits that define who they are, just as does ethnicity. For example, we know that homosexuality is 'immutable' insofar as it is highly resistant to attempts to change it, such as the various 'therapies' we have discussed in previous chapters. Therefore in an ideal world one might argue that gay people should be accorded the same rights and freedoms as everyone else because they constitute a special 'kind' or biological class of human being. We believe that there is considerable truth and justice in this notion. However, this issue of 'immutability' is complicated because it overlaps with the issue of self-control. Something that is truly immutable implies a complete lack of self-control over the behaviour, and we know that one could always try and stop homosexual behaviour through some means or another. Threats of capital punishment in force in some countries no doubt curtail homosexual displays and practices to some extent, as would anti-libido drugs, like cyproterone acetate, that are sometimes used to treat sex offenders such as rapists and paedophiles. However, neither of these extreme measures actually alters sexual orientation – they merely suppress its manifestation, and the fact that homosexual *feelings* cannot be reversed or totally eliminated shows they are completely natural for gay people. Same-sex behaviours are thus compelling and legitimate actions of gay people acting on internally hard-wired preferences, just as heterosexual feelings and activity are for heterosexuals.

Unfortunately, an immutability argument may not be wholly relevant to legal action or social policy. It can be easily argued that the observation that a given trait of a minority human population is biologically determined has little to do with whether that population should be treated differently. For example, ethnic minorities can claim an obvious biological basis for their difference, yet this has done little to eliminate racial prejudice in some societies. Thus whether homosexuality is biologically determined or not does not guarantee its social acceptance or rejection, the establishment of equal rights in terms of marriage, freedom from discrimination at work and so on. This, however, is a question about the future – whether accumulating more biological evidence on sexual orientation will actually make a difference to the lot of gay people. To this we answer 'we don't know', but we believe that any difference it does make is more likely to be positive than detrimental to the gay cause. That may well turn out to have little to do with science at the end of the day and more to do with that future society's attitudes towards human sexuality.

Earlier in the book we mentioned a parallel with handedness that is worthy of elaboration. Left-handedness is a minority condition that was once put down to accidental learning or deliberate cussedness, but is now known to be biologically determined and genetically influenced. At the height of the influence of environmentalist psychology in the 1950s it was argued that since left-handers would be at a disadvantage in a right-handed world (all instruments ranging from can-openers to pianos being designed for right-handers) then left-handedness should be corrected at an early age. Punishing regimes were introduced in many Anglo-American schools, forcing left-handed children to write, throw and perform various other skills with their right hands. This was, of course, a complete failure and was ultimately abandoned. Today we regard this as a cruel and unnecessary experiment; we recognize left-handedness as a natural variation and manufacture tools and equipment specifically for the use of left-handers. We still use the word 'sinister' to mean evil but we forget its etymology and do not expect left-handers to be any more malevolent than the rest of us. In short, recognition that handedness is hard-wired seems to have increased social acceptance of it; in certain sporting fields it even seems to be advantageous.

Perhaps something similar is happening with homosexuality. We no longer classify it as a disease and would not consider attempting crude aversion therapy techniques with electric shocks and emetics to eliminate it (as, again, was sometimes done in the 1950s). In fact, within a few decades in the UK we have gone from a state where homosexuality was illegal and punishable by prison, to one where sanctions are applied to those whose discriminate against people on grounds of their sexuality (e.g. in the field of employment). Of course, there are still plenty of quarters in which homosexuality is derided and detested, so there is still some way to go before it is as fully accepted as left-handedness.

Two of the most commonly voiced criticisms, especially from homophobic sources, are: (1) that homosexual practices spread diseases like AIDS, and (2) that they are not reproductive and hence counter to the divine purpose of sexual congress. With respect to the first, it is clear that all forms of sexual intercourse carry health dangers of which we need to be aware. Although AIDS may have first been detected in the homosexual community, heterosexual transmission is the main concern today. As for the link between sex and reproduction, it is clear that the course of evolution, through to our nearest relative the bonobo, is one of disentangling the two so as to appreciate their separate virtues. Claiming that sex was ordained for the purpose of having children is an argument equivalent to saying that if God had meant us to fly he would have equipped us with wings. Gay and lesbian people may be less reproductive than heterosexual people, but we live in an overcrowded world anyway, and they certainly cannot be accused of being less productive. On the contrary, the contribution of gay and lesbian people over the centuries to science, music, art, literature, politics and philanthropy has been outstanding.

REFERENCES

Adams, H.E., Wright, L.W. and Lohr, B.A. (1996) 'Is homophobia associated with homosexual arousal?' *Journal of Abnormal Psychology*, 105, pp. 440–45

Alexander, J.E. and Sufka, K.J. (1993) 'Cerebral lateralization in homosexual males: a preliminary EEG investigation', *International Journal of Psychophysiology*, 15, pp. 269–74

Allen, L.S. and Gorski, R.A. (1990) 'Sex differences in the bed nucleus of the stria terminalis of the human brain', *Journal of Comparative Neurology*, 302, pp. 697–706

Allen, L.S. and Gorski, R.A. (1991) 'Sexual dimorphism of the anterior commissure and massa intermedia of the human brain', *Journal of Comparative Neurology*, 312, pp. 97–104

Allen, L.S. and Gorski, R.A. (1992) 'Sexual orientation and the size of the anterior commissure in the human brain', *Proceedings of the National Academy of Sciences, USA*, 89, pp. 7199–202

Allen, L.S., Hines, M., Shryne, J.E. and Gorski, R.A. (1989) 'Two sexually dimorphic cell groups in the human brain', *Journal of Neuroscience*, 9, pp. 497–506

Allen, L.S., Richey, M.F., Chui, Y.M. and Gorski, R.A. (1991) 'Sex differences in the corpus callosum of the living human brain', *Journal of Neuroscience*, 11, pp. 933–42

Bagemihl, B. (1999) *Biological Exuberance: Animal Homosexuality and Natural Diversity*, New York, NY: St Martins Press

Bailey, J.M. (2003) *The Man Who Would Be Queen*, Washington, DC: Joseph Henry Press

Bailey, J.M., Barbow, P., Wolfe, M. and Mikach, S. (1995) 'Sexual orientation of adult sons of gay fathers', *Developmental Psychology*, 31, pp. 124–9

Bailey, J.M., Bechtold, K.T. and Berenbaum, S.A. (2002) 'Who are tomboys and why should we study them?', *Archives of Sexual Behavior*, 31, pp. 333–41

Bailey, J.M. and Bell, A.P. (1993) 'Familiality of female and male homosexuality', *Behavior Genetics*, 23, pp. 313–22

Bailey, J.M. and Benishay, B.A. (1993) 'Familial aggregation of female sexual orientation', *American Journal of Psychiatry*, 150, pp. 272–7

Bailey, J.M., Dunne, M.P. and Martin, N.G. (2000) 'Genetic and environmental influences on sexual orientation and its correlates in an Australian twin sample', *Journal of Personality and Social Psychology*, 78, pp. 524–36

Bailey, J.M., Gaulin, S., Agyei, Y. and Gladue, B.A. (1994) 'Effects of gender and sexual orientation on evolutionarily relevant aspects of human mating psychology', *Journal of Personality and Social Psychology*, 66, pp. 1081–93

Bailey, J.M., Kim, P.Y., Hills, A. and Linsenmeier, J.A.W. (1997) 'Butch, femme or straight acting? Partner preferences of gay men and lesbians', *Journal of Personality and Social Psychology*, 73, pp. 960–73

Bailey, J.M. and Pillard, R.C. (1991) 'A genetic study of male sexual orientation', *Archives of General Psychiatry*, 48, pp. 1089–96

Bailey, J.M., Pillard, R.C., Dawood, K., Miller, M.B., Farrer, L.A., Trivedi, S. and Murphy, R.L. (1999) 'A family history study of male sexual orientation using three independent samples', *Behavior Genetics*, 29, pp. 79–86

Bailey, J.M., Pillard, R.C., Neale, M.C. and Agyei, Y. (1993) 'Heritable factors influence sexual orientation in women', *Archives of General Psychiatry*, 50, pp. 217–23

Bailey, J.M., Willerman, L. and Parks, C. (1991) 'A test of the prenatal stress theory of human male homosexuality', *Archives of Sexual Behavior*, 20, pp. 277–93

Bailey, J.M. and Zucker, K.J. (1995) 'Childhood sex-typed behaviour and sexual orientation: a conceptual analysis and quantitative review', *Developmental Psychology*, 31, pp. 43–55

Baker, R.R. and Bellis, M.A. (1995) *Human Sperm Competition: Copulation, Masturbation and Fidelity*, London: Chapman & Hall

Bakker, J. and Slob, A.K. (1997) 'Sexual differentiation of the brain and partner preference in the male rat: behavioural, neuroanatomical and neuroimmunocytochemical studies', In Ellis, L. and Ebertz, L. (eds) *Sexual Orientation: Toward Biological Understanding*. Westport, CT: Praeger Press

Baumeister, R.F. (2000) 'Gender differences in erotic plasticity: the female sex drive as socially flexible and responsive', *Psychological Bulletin*, 126, pp. 347–74

Bauserman, R. and Rind, B. (1997) 'Psychological correlates of male child and adolescent sexual experience with adults: a review of the nonclinical literature', *Archives of Sexual Behavior*, 26, pp. 105–42

Bell, A.P. and Weinberg, M. (1978) *Homosexualities: A Study of Diversity Among Men and Women*, New York, NY: Simon & Schuster

Bell, A.P., Weinberg, M. and Hammersmith, S.K. (1981) *Sexual Preference: Its Development in Men and Women*, Bloomington, IN: Indiana University Press

Bem, D.J. (1996) 'Exotic becomes erotic: a developmental theory of sexual orientation', *Psychological Review*, 103, pp. 320–35

Berenbaum, S.A. (1999) 'Effects of early androgens on sex-typed activities and interests in adolescents with congenital adrenal hyperplasia', *Hormones and Behavior*, 35, pp. 102–10

Berenbaum, S.A. and Hines, M. (1992) 'Early androgens are related to childhood sex-typed toy preferences', *Psychological Science*, 3, pp. 203–6

Berenbaum, S.A. and Snyder, E. (1995) 'Early hormonal influences on childhood sex-typed activity and playmate preferences: implications for the development of sexual orientation', *Developmental Psychology*, 31, pp. 31–42

Blanchard, R. (1997) 'Birth order and sibling sex ratio in homosexual versus heterosexual males and females', *Annual Review of Sex Research*, 8, pp. 27–67

Blanchard, R. (2001) 'Fraternal birth order and the maternal immune hypothesis of male homosexuality', *Hormones and Behavior*, 40, pp. 105–14

Blanchard, R. (2004) 'Quantitative and theoretical analyses of the relation between older brothers and homosexuality in men', *Journal of Theoretical Biology*, 230, pp. 173–87

Blanchard, R. and Bogaert, A.F. (1996a) 'Homosexuality in men and number of older brothers', *American Journal of Psychiatry*, 153, pp. 27–31

Blanchard, R. and Bogaert, A.F. (1996b) 'Biodemographic comparisons of homosexual and heterosexual men in the Kinsey interview data', *Archives of Sexual Behavior*, 25, pp. 551–79

Blanchard, R. and Bogaert, A.F. (1997) 'Additive effects of older brothers and homosexual brothers in the prediction of marriage and cohabitation', *Behavior Genetics*, 27, pp. 45–54

Blanchard, R. and Bogaert, A.F. (2004) 'Proportion of homosexual men who owe their sexual orientation to fraternal birth order: an estimate based on two national probability samples', *American Journal of Human Biology*, 16, pp. 151–7

Blanchard, R. and Ellis, L. (2001) 'Birth weight, sexual orientation and the sex of preceding siblings', *Journal of Biosocial Science*, 33, pp. 451–67

Blanchard, R. and Klassen, P. (1997) 'H-Y antigen and homosexuality in men', *Journal of Theoretical Biology*, 185, pp. 373–8

Blanchard, R. and Sheridan, P.M. (1992) 'Sibship size, sibling sex ratio, birth order, and parental age in homosexual and non-homosexual gender dysphorics', *Journal of Nervous and Mental Disease*, 180, pp. 40–7

Blanchard, R., Zucker, K.J., Bradley, S.J. and Humen, C.S. (1995) 'Birth order and sibling sex ratio in homosexual male adolescents and probably pre-homosexual feminine boys', *Developmental Psychology*, 31, pp. 22–30

Blanchard, R., Zucker, K.J., Cavacas, A., Allin, S., Bradley, S.J. and Schachter, D.C. (2002) 'Fraternal birth order and birth weight in probably prehomosexual feminine boys', *Hormones and Behavior*, 41, pp. 321–7

Blanchard, R., Zucker, K.J., Siegelman, M., Dickey, R. and Klassen, P. (1998) 'The relation of birth order to sexual orientation in men and women', *Journal of Biosocial Science*, 30, pp. 511–19

Bobrow, D. and Bailey, J.M. (2001) 'Is male homosexuality maintained via kin selection?', *Evolution and Human Behavior*, 22, pp. 361–8

Bogaert, A.F. (1997) 'Birth order and sexual orientation in women', *Behavioral Neuroscience*, 11, pp. 1395–7

Bogaert, A.F. (1998a) 'Physical development and sexual orientation in women: height, weight and age of puberty comparisons', *Personality and Individual Differences*, 24, pp. 115–21

Bogaert, A.F. (1998b) 'Birth order and sibling sex ratio in homosexual and heterosexual non-white men', *Archives of Sexual Behavior*, 27, pp. 467–73

Bogaert, A.F. (2000) 'Birth order and sexual orientation in a national probability sample', *Journal of Sex Research*, 37, pp. 361–8

Bogaert, A.F. (2003) 'Number of older brothers and sexual orientation: new tests and the attraction/behaviour distinction in two national probability samples', *Journal of Personality and Social Psychology*, 84, pp. 644–52

Bogaert, A.F. and Blanchard, R. (1996) 'Physical development and sexual orientation in men: height, weight and age of puberty differences', *Personality and Individual Differences*, 21, pp. 77–84

Bogaert, A.F. and Friesen, C. (2002) 'Sexual orientation and height, weight, and age of puberty: new tests from a British national probability sample', *Biological Psychology*, 59, pp. 135–45

Bogaert, A.F., Friesen, C. and Klentrou, P. (2002) 'Age of puberty and sexual orientation in a national probability sample', *Archives of Sexual Behavior*, 31, pp. 73–81

Bogaert, A.F. and Herschberger, S. (1999) 'The relation between sexual orientation and penile size', *Archives of Sexual Behavior*, 28, pp. 213–21

Bradley, S.J., Oliver, G.D., Chernick, A.B. and Zucker, K.J. (1998) 'Experiment of nurture: ablatio penis at 2 months, sex reassignment at 7 months, and a psychosexual follow-up in young adulthood', *Pediatrics*, 102: http://www.pediatrics.org/cgi/content/full/102/1/e9

Brown, W.M., Finn, C.J., Cooke, B.M. and Breedlove, S.M. (2002) 'Differences in finger-length ratios between self-identified 'butch' and 'femme' lesbians', *Archives of Sexual Behavior*, 31, pp. 123–7

Brown, W.M., Hines, M., Fane, B. and Breedlove, S.M (2002) 'Masculinised finger-length ratios in humans with congenital adrenal hyperplasia', *Hormones and Behavior*, 42, pp. 380–6

Buhrich, N. and McConaghy, N. (1978) 'Parental relationships during childhood in homosexuality, transvestism and transsexuality', *Australian and New Zealand Journal of Psychiatry*, 12, pp. 103–8

Byne, W. (1998) 'The medial preoptic and anterior hypothalamic regions of the rhesus monkey: cytoarchitectonic comparison with the human and evidence of sexual dimorphism', *Brain Research*, 793, pp. 346–50

Byne, W., Lasco, M.S., Kemether, E., Shinwari, A., Edgar, M.A., Morgello, S., Jones, L.B. and Tobet, S. (2000) 'The interstitial nuclei of the human anterior hypothalamus: an investigation of sexual variation in volume and cell size, number and density', *Brain Research*, 856, pp. 254–8

Byne, W., Tobet, S., Mattiace, L.A., Lasco, M.S., Kemether, E., Edgar, M.A., Morgello, S., Buchsbaum, M.S. and Jones, L.B. (2001) 'The interstitial nuclei of the human anterior hypothalamus: an investigation of variation with sex, sexual orientation and HIV status', *Hormones and Behavior*, 40, pp. 86–92

Cameron, P. and Cameron, K. (1995) 'Does incest cause homosexuality?', *Psychological Report*, 76, pp. 611–21

Campbell, A. (1999) 'Staying alive: evolution, culture and women's intrasexual aggression', *Behavioural and Brain Sciences*, 22, pp. 203–412

Cantor, J.M., Blanchard, R., Paterson, A.D. and Bogaert, A.F. (2002) 'How many gay men owe their sexual orientation to fraternal birth order?', *Archives of Sexual Behavior*, 31, pp. 63–71

Celotti, F., Melcangi, R.C. and Martini, L. (1992) 'The 5 alpha reductase in the brain: molecular aspects and relation to brain function', *Frontiers in Neuroendocrinology*, 13, pp. 163–215

Chivers, M.L., Rieger, G., Latty, E. and Bailey, J.M. (in press) 'A sex difference in the specificity of sexual arousal', *Psychological Science*

Clark, M.M., Robertson, R.K. and Galef, B.G., Jr (1996) 'Effects of perinatal testosterone on handedness of gerbils: support for part of the Geschwind-Galaburda hypothesis', *Behavioral Neuroscience*, 110, pp. 413–17

Collaer, M.L. and Hines, M. (1995) 'Human behavioral sex differences: a role for gonadal hormones during early development?', *Psychological Bulletin*, 118, pp. 55–107

Condy, S., Templer, D., Brown, R. and Veaco, L. (1987) 'Parameters of sexual contact of boys with women', *Archives of Sexual Behavior*, 16, pp. 379–94

Cooke, B., Hegstrom, C.D., Villeneuve, L.S. and Breedlove, S.M. (1998) 'Sexual differentiation of the vertebrate brain: principles and mechanisms', *Frontiers in Neuroendocrinology*, 19, pp. 253–86

Cooke, B.M., Tabibnia, G. and Breedlove, S.M. (1999) 'A brain sexual dimorphism controlled by adult circulating androgens', *Proceedings of the National Academy of Sciences, USA*, 96, pp. 7538–40

Copas, A.J., Wellings, K., Erens, B., Mercer, C.H., McManus, S., Fenton, K.A., Korovessis, C., Macdowall, W., Nanchahal, K. and Johnson, A.M. (2002) 'The accuracy of reported sensitive sexual behaviour in Britain: exploring the extent of change 1990–2000', *Sexually Transmitted Infections*, 78, pp. 26–30

Corliss, H.L., Cochran, S.D. and Mays, V.M. (2002) 'Reports of parental maltreatment during childhood in a United States population-based survey of homosexual, bisexual, and heterosexual adults', *Child Abuse and Neglect*, 26, pp. 1165–78

Cowell, P.E., Kertesz, A. and Deneberg, V.H. (1993) 'Multiple dimensions of handedness and the human corpus callosum', *Neurology*, 43, pp. 2353–7

Dancey, C.P. (1990) 'Sexual orientation in women: an investigation of hormonal and personality variables', *Biological Psychology*, 30, pp. 251–64

Davis, E.C., Shryne, J.E. and Gorski, R.A. (1995) 'A revised critical period for the sexual differentiation of the sexual dimorphic nucleus of the preoptic area in the rat', *Neuroendocrinology*, 62, pp. 579–85

Dawood, K., Pillard, R.C., Horvath, C., Revelle, W. and Bailey, J.M. (2000) 'Familial aspects of male homosexuality', *Archives of Sexual Behavior*, 29, pp. 155–63

Diamond, L.M. (2003) 'Was it a phase? Young women's relinquishment of lesbian/bisexual identities over a 5-year period', *Journal of Personality and Social Psychology*, 84, pp. 352–64

Diamond, M. (1982) 'Sexual identity, monozygotic twins reared in discordant sex roles and a BBC follow-up', *Archives of Sexual Behavior*, 11, pp. 181–6

Diamond, M. and Sigmundson, H.K. (1997) 'Sex reassignment at birth: long-term review and clinical implications', *Archives of Pediatric and Adolescent Medicine*, 151, pp. 298–304

Dickson, N., Paul, C. and Herbison, P. (2003) 'Same-sex attraction in a birth cohort: prevalence and persistence in early adulthood', *Social Science and Medicine*, 56, pp. 1607–15

Dittman, R.W., Kappes, M.E. and Happes, M.H. (1992) 'Sexual behavior in adolescent and adult females with congenital adrenal hyperplasia', *Psychoneuroendocrinology*, 17, pp. 153–70

Dorner, G., Geier, T., Ahrens, L., Krell, L., Munx, G., Sieler, H., Kittner, E. and Muller, H. (1980) 'Prenatal stress as possible etiogenic factor of homosexuality in human males', *Endokrinologie*, 75, pp. 365–8

Dorner, G., Schenk, B., Schmiedel, B. and Ahrens, L. (1983) 'Stressful events in prenatal life of bi- and homosexual men', *Experimental and Clinical Endocrinology*, 81, 83–7

Dunn, J. and Plomin, R. (1990) *Separate Lives: Why Siblings Are So Different*, New York, NY: Basic Books

DuPree, M.G., Mustanski, B.S., Bocklandt, S., Nievergelt, C. and Hamer, D.H. (2004) 'A candidate gene study of CYP19 (aromatase) and male sexual orientation', *Behavior Genetics*, 34, pp. 243–50

Ehrhardt, A.A., Meyer-Bahlburg, H.F.L., Rosen, L.R., Feidman, J.F., Veridiano, N.P., Zimmerman, I. and McEwen, B.S. (1985) 'Sexual orientation after prenatal exposure to exogenous estrogen', *Archives of Sexual Behavior*, 14, pp. 57–77

Ellis, L. and Ames, M.A. (1987) 'Neurohormonal functioning and sexual orientation: a theory of homosexuality–heterosexuality', *Psychological Bulletin*, 101, pp. 233–58

Ellis, L. and Blanchard, R. (2001) 'Birth order, sibling sex ratio, and maternal miscarriages in homosexual and heterosexual men and women', *Personality and Individual Differences*, 30, pp. 543–52

Ellis, L. and Cole-Harding, S. (2001) 'The effects of prenatal stress, and of prenatal alcohol and nicotine exposure, on human sexual orientation', *Physiology and Behavior*, 74, pp. 1–14

Ellis, L. and Hellberg, J. (2005) 'Fetal exposure to prescription drugs and adult sexual orientation', *Personality and Individual Differences*, 38, pp. 225–36

Erens, B., McManus, S., Prescott, A., Field, J., Johnson, A.M., Wellings, K., Fenton, K.A., Mercer, C., Macdowell, W., Copas, A.J. and Nanchahal, K. (2003) *National Survey of Sexual Attitudes and Lifestyles II. References Table and Summary Reports*, London: National Centre for Social Research

Ernst, C. and Angst, J. (1983) *Birth Order: Its Influence on Personality*, Berlin: Springer-Verlag

Everitt, B.J. (1990) 'Sexual motivation: a neural and behavioral analysis of the mechanisms underlying appetitive and copulatory responses of male rats', *Neuroscience and Biobehavioral Reviews*, 14, pp. 217–32

Eysenck, H.J. and Wilson, G.D. (1973) *The Experimental Study of Freudian Theories*, London: Methuen

Fernandez-Guasti, A., Kruijver, F.P.M., Fodor, M. and Swaab, D.F. (2000) 'Sex differences in the distribution of androgen receptors in the human hypothalamus', *Journal of Comparative Neurology*, 425, pp. 422–35

Finegan, J.K., Zucker, K.J., Bradley, S.J. and Doering, R.W. (1982) 'Patterns of intellectual functioning and spatial ability in boys with gender identity disorder', *Canadian Journal of Psychiatry*, 27, pp. 135–9

Forastieri, V., Andrade, C.P., Souza, A.L.V., Silva, M.S., El-Hani, C.N., Moreira, L.M.d.A., Mott, L.R.d.B. and Flores, R.Z. (2003) 'Evidence against a relationship between dermatoglyphic asymmetry and male sexual orientation', *Human Biology*, 74, pp. 861–70

Freud, S. (2000) *Three Essays on the Theory of Sexuality* (tr. J. Strachey), New York, NY: Basic Books; first publication 1905

Freund, K. (1963) 'A laboratory method for diagnosing predominance of homo- or hetero-erotic interest in the male', *Behaviour Research and Therapy*, 1, pp. 85–93

Freund, K. and Blanchard, R. (1983) 'Is the distant relationship of fathers of homosexual sons related to the sons' erotic preference for male partners, or to the sons' atypical gender identity, or to both?', *Journal of Homosexuality*, 9, pp. 7–25

Freund, K., Watson, R. and Rienzo, D. (1989) 'Heterosexuality, homosexuality, and erotic age preference', *Journal of Sex Research*, 26, pp. 107–17

Gangestad, S.W., Bailey, J.M. and Martin, N.G. (2000) 'Taxometric analyses of sexual orientation and gender identity', *Journal of Personality and Social Psychology*, 78, pp. 1109–21

Geschwind, N. and Galaburda, A.M. (1985a) 'Cerebral lateralisation, biological mechanisms, associations, and pathology: I. A hypothesis and a program for research', *Archives of Neurology*, 42, pp. 428–59

Geschwind, N. and Galaburda, A.M. (1985b) 'Cerebral lateralisation, biological mechanisms, associations, and pathology: II. A hypothesis and program for research', *Archives of Neurology*, 42, pp. 521–52

Getz, W.M. (1993) 'Invasion and maintenance of alleles that influence mating and parental success', *Journal of Theoretical Biology*, 162, pp. 515–37

Gladue, B.A. and Bailey, J.M. (1995) 'Aggressiveness, competitiveness and human sexual orientation', *Psychoneuroendocrinology*, 20, pp. 475–85

Gladue, B.A., Beatty, W.W., Larson, J. and Staton, R.D. (1990) 'Sexual orientation and spatial ability in men and women', *Psychobiology*, 18, pp. 101–8

Golombok, S., Spencer, A. and Rutter, M. (1983) 'Children in lesbian and single-parent households: psychosexual and psychiatric appraisal', *Journal of Child Psychology and Psychiatry*, 24, pp. 551–72

Golombok, S. and Tasker, F. (1996) 'Do parents influence the sexual orientation of their children? Findings from a longitudinal study of lesbian families', *Developmental Psychology*, 32, pp. 3–11

Gorski, R.A., Gordon, J.H., Shryne, J.E. and Southam, A.M. (1978) 'Evidence for a morphological sex difference within the medial preoptic area of the rat brain', *Brain Research*, 148, pp. 333–46

Goy, R.W., Bercovitch, F.B. and McBrair, M.C. (1988) 'Behavioral masculinization is independent of genital masculinization in prenatally androgenized female rhesus macaques', *Hormones and Behavior*, 22, pp. 552–71

Green, R. (1987) *The Sissy Boy Syndrome and the Development of Homosexuality*, New Haven, CT: Yale University Press

Green, R. (2000) 'Birth order and ratio of brothers to sisters in transsexuals', *Psychological Medicine*, 30, pp. 789–95

Green, R. and Young, R. (2000) 'Fingerprint asymmetry in male and female transsexuals', *Personality and Individual Differences*, 29, pp. 933–42

Greenberg, A.S. and Bailey, J.M. (1993) 'Do biological explanations of homosexuality have moral, legal and policy implications?', *Journal of Sex Research*, 30, pp. 245–51

Grimshaw, G.M., Zucker, K.J., Bradley, S.J., Lowry, C.B. and Mitchell, J.N. (1991) 'Verbal and spatial ability in boys with gender identity disorder', poster presented at the International Academy of Sex Research, Ontario, Canada, August 1991

Gualtieri, T. and Hicks, R.E. (1985) 'An immunoreactive theory of selective male affliction', *Behavioral and Brain Sciences*, 8, pp. 427–41

Habib, M., Gayraud, D., Oliva, A., Regis, J., Salamon, G. and Khalil, R. (1991) 'Effects of handedness and sex on the morphology of the corpus callosum: a study with brain magnetic resonance imaging', *Brain and Cognition*, 16, pp. 41–61

Hall, J.A.Y. and Kimura, D. (1994) 'Dermatoglyphic asymmetry and sexual orientation in men', *Behavioral Neuroscience*, 108, pp. 1203–6

Hall, J.A.Y. and Kimura, D. (1995) 'Performance by homosexual males and females on sexually dimorphic motor tasks', *Archives of Sexual Behavior*, 24, pp. 395–407

Hamer, D.H. (1999) 'Genetics and male sexual orientation', *Science*, 285, pp. 803.

Hamer, D. and Copeland, P. (1994) *The Science of Desire*, New York, NY: Simon & Schuster

Hamer, D.H., Hu, S., Magnuson, V.L., Hu, N. and Pattatucci, A.M.L. (1993) 'A linkage between DNA markers on the X chromosome and male sexual orientation', *Science*, 261, pp. 321–7

Harris, J.R. (1998) *The Nurture Assumption: Why Children Turn Out the Way They Do*, New York, NY: Free Press

Helle, S., Lummaa, V. and Jokela, J. (2002) 'Sons reduced maternal longevity in pre-industrial humans', *Science*, 296, p. 108

Herdt, G. (1981) *Guardians of the Flutes: Idioms of Masculinity*, New York, NY: Columbia University Press

Herman, R.A., Jones, B., Mann, D.R. and Wallen, K. (2000) 'Timing of prenatal androgen exposure: anatomical and endocrine effects on juvenile male and female rhesus monkeys', *Hormones and Behavior*, 38, pp. 52–66

Hines, M. (2000) 'Gonadal hormones and sexual differentiation of human behavior: effects on psychosexual and cognitive development', in Matsumoto, A. (ed.), *Sexual Differentiation of the Brain*, Boca Raton, FL: CRC Press

Hines, M., Ahmed, S.F. and Hughes, I.A. (2003) 'Psychological outcomes and gender related development in complete androgen insensitivity syndrome', *Archives of Sexual Behavior*, 32, pp. 93–101

Hines, M., Johnston, K.J., Golombok, S., Rust, J., Stevens, M., Golding, J. and the ALSPAC Study Team (2002) 'Prenatal stress and gender role behavior in girls and boys: a longitudinal, population study', *Hormones and Behavior*, 42, pp. 126–34

Hiscock, M., Inch, R., Jacek, C., Hiscock-Kalil, C. and Kalil, K.M. (1994) 'Is there a sex difference in human laterality? I. An exhaustive survey of auditory laterality studies from six neuropsychology journals', *Journal of Clinical and Experimental Neuropsychology*, 16, pp. 423–35

Hiscock, M., Israelian, M., Inch, R., Jacek, C. and Kalil-Hiscock, C. (1995) 'Is there a sex difference in human laterality? II. An exhaustive survey of visual laterality studies from six neuropsychology journals', *Journal of Clinical and Experimental Neuropsychology*, 17, pp. 590–610

Houtsmuller, E.J., Brand, T., de Jonger, F.H., Joosten, R.N., van de Poll, N.E. and Slob, A.K. (1994) 'SDN-POA volume, sexual behavior, and partner preference in male rats affected by perinatal treatment with ATD', *Physiology and Behavior*, 56, pp. 535–41

Howard, R.C. (1995) 'The neurophysiology of sexual desire, with particular reference to paedophilia', *Annals for the Academy of Medicine of Singapore*, 24, pp. 724–7

Hu, S., Pattatucci, A.M.L., Patterson, C., Li, L., Fulker, D.W., Cherny, S.S., Kruglyak, L. and Hamer, D.H. (1995) 'Linkage between sexual orientation and chromosome Xq28 in males but not in females', *Nature Genetics*, 11, pp. 248–56

Isay, R.A. (1989) *Being Homosexual: Gay Men and Their Development*, New York, NY: Farrar, Straus and Giroux

Jamison, C.S., Jamison, P.L. and Meier, R.J. (1994) 'Effect of prenatal testosterone administration on palmar dermatoglyphic intercore ridge counts of rhesus monkeys (Macaca mulata)', *American Journal of Physical Anthropology*, 94, pp. 409–19

Johnson, A.M., Mercer, C.H., Erens, B., Copas, A.J., McManus, S., Wellings, K., Fenton, K.A., Korovessis, C., Macdowall, W., Nanchahal, K., Purdon, S. and Field, J. (2001) 'Sexual behaviour in Britain: partnerships, practices and HIV risk behaviours', *The Lancet*, 358, pp. 1835–42

Jones, M.B. and Blanchard, R. (1998) 'Birth order and male homosexuality: an extension of Slater's index', *Human Biology*, 70, pp. 775–87

Kallmann, F.J. (1952) Comparative twin studies on genetic aspects of male homosexuality. *Journal of Nervous and Mental Disease*, 115, pp. 283–98

Karama, S., Lecours, A.R., Lerous, J-M., Bourgouin, P., Beaudoin, G., Joubert, S. and Beauregard, M. (2002) 'Areas of brain activation in males and females during viewing of erotic film excerpts', *Human Brain Mapping*, 16, pp. 1–13

Kendler, K.S., Thornton, L.M., Gilman, S.E. and Kessler, R.C. (2000) 'Sexual orientation in a US national sample of twin and non-twin sibling pairs', *American Journal of Psychiatry*, 157, pp. 1843–6

Kimura, D. (1999) *Sex and Cognition*, Cambridge, MA: MIT Press

Kindon, H.A., Baum, M.J. and Paredes, R.J. (1996) 'Medial preoptic/anterior hypothalamic lesions induce a female-typical profile of sexual partner preference in male ferrets', *Hormones and Behavior*, 30, pp. 514–27

Kinnunen, L.H., Moltz, H., Metz, J. and Copper, M. (2003) 'Differential brain activation in exclusively homosexual and heterosexual men produced by an SSRI', Society for Neuroscience Annual Meeting, New Orleans, November

Kinsey, A.C., Pomeroy, W.B. and Martin, C.E. (1948) *Sexual Behavior in the Human Male*, Philadelphia, PA: Saunders

Kinsey, A.C., Pomeroy, W.B., Martin, C.E. and Gebhard, P.H. (1953) *Sexual Behavior in the Human Female*, Philadelphia, PA: Saunders

Kirk, K.M., Bailey, J.M., Dunne, M.P. and Martin, N.G. (2000) 'Measurement models for sexual orientation in a community twin sample', *Behavior Genetics*, 30, 345–56

Kirk, K.M., Bailey, J.M. and Martin, N.G. (1999) 'How accurate is the family history method for assessing siblings sexual orientation?', *Archives of Sexual Behavior*, 28, pp. 129–38

Kirkpatrick, R.C. (2000) 'The evolution of homosexual behavior', *Current Anthropology*, 41, pp. 385–413

Kruijver, F.P.M., Fernandez-Guasti, A., Fodor, M., Kraan, E.M. and Swaab, D.F. (2001) 'Sex differences in androgen receptors of the human mamillary bodies are related to endocrine status rather than to sexual orientation and transsexuality', *Journal of Clinical Endocrinology and Metabolism*, 86, pp. 818–27

Kruijver, F.P.M., Zhou, J.N., Pool, C.W., Hofman, M.A., Gooren, L.J.G. and Swaab, D.F. (2000) 'Male to female transsexuals have female neuron numbers in a limbic nucleus', *Journal of Clinical Endocrinology and Metabolism*, 85, pp. 2034–41

Lalumiere, M.L., Blanchard, R. and Zucker, K.J. (2000) 'Sexual orientation and handedness in men and women: a meta-analysis', *Psychological Bulletin*, 126, pp. 575–92

Lasco, M.S., Jordan, T.J., Edgar, M.A., Petito, C.K. and Byne, W. (2002) 'A lack of dimorphism of sex or sexual orientation in the human anterior commissure', *Brain Research*, 936, pp. 95–8

Laumann, E.O., Michael, R.T., Gagnon, J.H. and Michaels, S. (1994) *The Social Organization of Sexuality: Sexual Practices in the United States*, Chicago, IL: University of Chicago Press

LeVay, S. (1991) 'A difference in hypothalamic structure between heterosexual and homosexual men', *Science*, 253, pp. 1034–7

LeVay, S. (1993) *The Sexual Brain*, Cambridge, MA: MIT Press

LeVay, S. (1996) *Queer Science*, Cambridge, MA: MIT Press

Levy, J. and Heller, W. (1992) 'Gender differences in human neuropsychological function', in Gerall, A.A., Moltz, H. and Ward, I.L. (eds), *Sexual Differentiation: Handbook of Behavioral Neurology*, Vol. 11. New York, NY: Plenum Press

Lippa, R.A (2000) 'Gender-related traits in gay men, lesbian women, and heterosexual men and women: the virtual identity of homosexual-heterosexual diagnosticity and gender diagnosticity', *Journal of Personality*, 68, pp. 899–926

Lippa, R.A. (2002) 'Gender-related traits of heterosexual and homosexual men and women', *Archives of Sexual Behavior*, 31, pp. 83–98

Lippa, R.A. (2003) 'Are 2D:4D finger-length ratios related to sexual orientation? Yes for men, no for women', *Journal of Personality and Social Psychology*, 85, pp. 179–88

Lippa, R.A. and Hershberger, S. (1999) 'Genetic and environmental influences on individual differences in masculinity, femininity, and gender diagnosticity: analysing data from a classic twin study', *Journal of Personality*, 67, pp. 127–55

Lippa, R.A. and Tan, F.D. (2001) 'Does culture moderate the relationship between sexual orientation and gender-related personality traits?'. *Cross Cultural Research*, 35, pp. 65–87

Loulan, J. (1990) *The Lesbian Erotic Dance: Butch, Femme, Androgyny, and Other Rhythms*, San Francisco, CA: Spinsters Ink

Lutchmaya, S., Baron-Cohen, S., Raggatt, P., Knickmeyer, R., Manning, J.T. (2004) '2nd to 4th digit ratios, fetal testosterone and estradiol', *Early Human Development*, 77, pp. 23–8

MacIntrye, F. and Estep, K.W. (1993) 'Sperm competition and the persistence of the genes for male homosexuality', *Biosystems*, 31, pp. 223–33

Macke, J.P., Hu, N., Hu, S., Bailey, M., King, V.L., Brown, T., Hamer, D. and Nathans, J. (1993) 'Sequence variation in the androgen receptor gene is not a common determinant of male sexual orientation', *American Journal of Human Genetics*, 53, pp. 844–52

Manning, J.T. (2002) *Digit Ratio: A Pointer to Fertility, Behaviour and Health*, Piscataway, NJ: Rutgers University Press

Manning, J.T., Barley, L., Walton, J., Lewis-Jones, D.I., Trivers, R.L., Singh, D., Thornhill, R., Rohde, P., Bereczkei, T., Henzi, P., Soler, M. and Szwed, A. (2000) 'The 2nd:4th digit ratio, sexual dimorphism, population differences and reproductive success: evidence for sexually antagonistic genes?', *Evolution and Human Behavior*, 21, pp. 163–83

Manning, J.T., Bundred, P.E., Newton, D.J. and Flanagan, B.F. (2003) 'The second to fourth finger-length ratio and variation in the androgen receptor gene', *Evolution and Human Behavior*, 24, pp. 399–405

Manning, J.T. and Robinson, S.J. (2003) '2nd to 4th digit ratio and a universal mean for prenatal testosterone in homosexual men', *Medical Hypotheses*, 61, pp. 303–6

Manning, J.T., Scutt, D., Wilson, J. and Lewis-Jones, D.I. (1998) 'The ratio of the 2nd to 4th digit length: a predictor of sperm numbers and levels of testosterone, LH and oestrogen', *Human Reproduction*, 13, pp. 3000–4

Martensen-Larsen, O. (1957) 'The family constellation and homosexualism', *Acta Genetica et Statistica Medica*, 7, pp. 445–6

Martin, J.T. and Nguyen, D.H. (2004) 'Anthropometric analysis of homosexuals and heterosexuals: implications for early hormone exposure', *Hormones and Behavior*, 45, pp. 31–9

McCormick, C.M. and Witelson, S.F. (1991) 'A cognitive profile of homosexual men compared to heterosexual men and women', *Psychoneuroendocrinology*, 15, pp. 459–73

McCormick, C.M. and Witelson, S.F. (1994) 'Functional cerebral asymmetry and sexual orientation in men and women', *Behavioral Neuroscience*, 108, 525–31

McFadden, D. (1993) 'A masculinizing effect on the auditory systems of human females having male co-twins', *Proceedings of the National Academy of Sciences, USA*, 90, pp. 11900–4

McFadden, D. (2002) 'Masculinisation effects in the auditory systems', *Archives of Sexual Behavior*, 31, 99–111

McFadden, D. and Champlin, C.A. (2000) 'Comparison of auditory evoked potentials in heterosexual, homosexual and bisexual males and females', *Journal of the Association for Research in Otolaryngology*, 1, pp. 89–99

McFadden, D. and Pasanen, E.G. (1998) 'Comparison of the auditory systems of heterosexuals and homosexuals: click-evoked otoacoustic emissions', *Proceedings of the National Academy of Sciences, USA*, 95, pp. 2709–13

McFadden, D. and Pasanen, E.G. (1999) 'Spontaneous otoacoustic emissions in heterosexuals, homosexuals and bisexuals', *Journal of the Acoustical Society of America*, 105, pp. 2403–13

McFadden, D. and Schubel, E. (2002) 'Relative lengths of fingers and toes in human males and females', *Hormones and Behavior*, 42, pp. 492–500

McKnight, J. (1997) *Straight Science: Homosexuality, Evolution and Adaption*, London: Routledge

McKnight, J. and Malcolm, J. (2000) 'Is male homosexuality maternally linked?', *Psychology, Evolution and Gender*, 2, pp. 229–52

Meaney, M.J. and McEwen, B.S. (1986) 'Testosterone implants into the amygdala during the neonatal period masculinise the social play of juvenile male rats', *Brain Research*, 398, pp. 324–8

Meyer-Bahlburg, H.F.L. (1984) 'Psychoendocrine research on sexual orientation: current status and future options', *Progress in Brain Research*, 61, pp. 375–98

Meyer-Bahlburg, H.F.L., Ehrhardt, A.A., Rosen, L.R., Gruen, R.S., Veridiano, N.P., Vann, F.H. and Neuwalder, H.F. (1995) 'Prenatal estrogens and the development of homosexual orientation', *Developmental Psychology*, 31, pp. 12–21

Mikach, S.M. and Bailey, J.M. (1999) 'What distinguishes women with high numbers of sex partners', *Evolution and Human Behavior*, 20, pp. 141–50

Miller, E.M. (2000) 'Homosexuality, birth order and evolution: toward an equilibrium reproductive economics of homosexuality', *Archives of Sexual Behavior*, 29, pp. 1–34

Moffat, S.D., Hampson, E., Wickett, J.C., Vernon, P.A. and Lee, D.H. (1997) 'Testosterone is correlated with regional morphology of the human corpus callosum'. *Brain*, 767, pp. 297–304

Moller, A.P. and Swaddle, J.P. (1997) *Asymmetry, Developmental Stability and Evolution*, London: Oxford University Press

Money, J. (1975) 'Ablatio penis: normal male infant sex-reassigned as a girl', *Archives of Sexual Behavior*, 4, pp. 65–71

Money, J. (1988) *Gay, Straight and In-between: The Sexology of Erotic Arousal*, New York, NY: Oxford University Press

Money, J. and Ehrhardt, A.A. (1972) *Man and Woman, Boy and Girl: The Differentiation and Dimorphism of Gender Identity from Conception to Maturity*, Baltimore, MD: Johns Hopkins University Press

Money, J., Schwartz, M. and Lewis, V.G. (1984) 'Adult erotosexual status and fetal hormonal masculinisation and demasculinisation: 46, XX congenital virilizing adrenal hyperplasia and 46, XY androgen-insensitivity syndrome compared', *Psychoneuroendocrinology*, 9, pp. 405–14

Muscarella, F. (1999) 'The homoerotic behavior that never evolved', *Journal of Homosexuality*, 37, pp. 1–18

Muscarella, F. (2000) 'The evolution of homoerotic behavior in humans', *Journal of Homosexuality*, 40, pp. 51–77

Mustanski, B.S., Bailey, J.M. and Kaspar, S. (2002) 'Dermatoglyphics, handedness, sex and sexual orientation', *Archives of Sexual Behavior*, 31, pp. 113–22

Neave, N., Menaged, M. and Weightman, D.R. (1999) 'Sex differences in cognition: the role of testosterone and sexual orientation', *Brain and Cognition*, 41, pp. 245–62

Nedoma, K. and Freund, K. (1961) 'Somatosexulni nalezy u homosexualnich muzu [Somatosexual findings in homosexual men]', *Ceskoslovenska Psychiatre*, 57, pp. 100–3

Nyborg, H. (1994) 'The neuropsychology of sex-related differences in brain and specific abilities', in Vernon, P.A. (ed.), *The Neuropsychology of Individual Differences*. New York, NY: Academic Press

Paredes, R.G. and Baum, M.J. (1995) 'Altered sexual partner preference in male ferrets given excitotoxic lesions of the preoptic area/anterior hypothalamus', *Journal of Neuroscience*, 15, pp. 6619–30

Pattatucci, A.M.L. and Hamer, D.H. (1995) 'Development and familiality of sexual orientation in females', *Behavior Genetics*, 25, pp. 407–20

Patterson, C. (1992) 'Children of lesbian and gay parents', *Child Development*, 63, pp. 1025–42

Pearcy, S.M., Docherty, K.J. and Dabbs, J.M. (1996) 'Testosterone and sex role identification in lesbian couples', *Physiology and Behavior*, 60, pp. 1033–5

Pellis, S.M. (2002) 'Sex differences in play fighting revisited: traditional and non-traditional mechanisms of sexual differentiation in rats', *Archives of Sexual Behavior*, 31, pp. 17–26

Peplau, L.A., Garnets, L.D., Spalding, L.R., Conley, T.D. and Veniegas, R.C. (1998) 'A critique of Bem's "Exotic becomes erotic" theory of sexual orientation', *Psychological Review*, 105, pp. 387–94

Perkins, M.W. (1981) 'Female homosexuality and body build', *Archives of Sexual Behavior*, 10, pp. 337–45

Perret, D.I., Lee, K.J., Penton-Voak, I., Rowland, D., Yoshikawa, S., Burt, D.M., Henzi, S.P., Castles, D.L. and Akamatsu, S. (1998) 'Effects of sexual dimorphism on facial attractiveness', *Nature*, 394, pp. 884–7

Phoenix, C.H., Goy, R.W., Gerall, A.A. and Yong, W.C. (1959) 'Organizing action of prenatally administered testosterone propionate on the tissues mediating mating behavior in the female guinea pig', *Endocrinology*, 65, pp. 369–82

Pillard, R.C. and Bailey, J.M. (1998) 'Human sexual orientation has a heritable component', *Human Biology*, 70, pp. 347–65

Pillard, R.C. and Weinrich, J.D. (1986) 'Evidence of familial nature of male homosexuality', *Archives of General Psychiatry*, 43, 808–12

Pinker, S. (2002) *The Blank Slate: The Modern Denial of Human Nature*, Harmondsworth: Penguin

Poasa, K.H., Blanchard, R. and Zucker, K.J. (2004) 'Birth order in transgendered males from Polynesia: a quantitative study of Samoan *Fa'afafine*', *Journal of Sex and Marital Therapy*, 30, pp. 13–23

Purcell, D.W., Blanchard, R. and Zucker, K.J. (2000) 'Birth order in a contemporary sample of gay men', *Archives of Sexual Behavior*, 29, pp. 349–56

Rahman, Q., Abrahams, S. and Wilson, G.D. (2003) 'Sexual orientation related differences in verbal fluency', *Neuropsychology*, 17, pp. 240–46

Rahman, Q., Kumari, V. and Wilson, G.D. (2003) 'Sexual orientation related differences in pre-pulse inhibition of the human startle response', *Behavioral Neuroscience*, 117, pp. 1096–1102

Rahman, Q. and Silber, K. (2000) 'Sexual orientation and the sleep–wake cycle: a preliminary investigation', *Archives of Sexual Behavior*, 29, pp. 127–34

Rahman, Q. and Wilson, G.D. (2003a) 'Born gay? The psychobiology of human sexual orientation', *Personality and Individual Differences*, 34, pp. 1337–82

Rahman, Q. and Wilson, G.D. (2003b) 'Sexual orientation and the 2nd to 4th finger-length ratio: evidence for organising effects of sex hormones or developmental instability?', *Psychoneuroendocrinology*, 28, pp. 288–303

Rahman, Q. and Wilson, G.D. (2003c) 'Large sexual orientation related differences in performance on mental rotation and judgement of line orientation', *Neuropsychology*, 17, pp. 25–31

Rahman, Q., Wilson, G.D. and Abrahams, S. (2003) 'Sexual orientation related differences in spatial memory', *Journal of the International Neuropsychological Society*, 9, pp. 376–83

Rahman, Q., Wilson, G.D. and Abrahams, S. (2004a) 'Performance differences between adult heterosexual and homosexual men on the Digit-Symbol Substitution sub-test of the WAIS', *Journal of Clinical and Experimental Neuropsychology*, 26, pp. 141–8

Rahman, Q., Wilson, G.D. and Abrahams, S. (2004b) 'Sex, sexual orientation and the identification of positive and negative facial affect', *Brain and Cognition*, 54, 179–85

Rahman, Q., Wilson, G.D. and Abrahams, S. (2004c) 'Biosocial factors, sexual orientation and neurocognitive functioning', *Psychoneuroendocrinology*, 29, pp. 867–81

Reiner, W.G. and Gearhart, J.P. (2004) 'Discordant sexual identity in some genetic males with cloacal exstrophy assigned to female sex at birth', *New England Journal of Medicine*, 350, pp. 333–41

Reite, M., Sheeder, J., Richardson, D. and Teale, P. (1995) 'Cerebral laterality in homosexual males: preliminary communication using magnetoencephalography', *Archives of Sexual Behavior*, 24, pp. 585–93

Rhodes, G., Hickford, C. and Jeffrey, L. (2000) 'Sex typicality and attractiveness: are super male and super female faces super attractive?', *British Journal of Psychology*, 91, pp. 125–40

Rice, G., Anderson, C., Risch, N. and Ebers, G. (1999) 'Male homosexuality: absence of linkage to microsatellite markers at Xq28', *Science*, 284, pp. 665–7

Rice, W.R. (1992) 'Sexually antagonistic genes: experimental evidence', *Science*, 256, pp. 1436–9

Ridge, S.R. and Feeney, J.A. (1998) 'Relationship history and relationship attitudes in gay males and lesbians: attachment style and gender differences', *Australian and New Zealand Journal of Psychiatry*, 32, pp. 848–59

Rieger, G., Chivers, M.L. and Bailey, J.M. (unpublished MS) 'In search of the elusive male bisexual: sexual arousal patterns in putatively bisexual men'

Rind, B. (1998) 'A meta-analytic examination of assumed properties of child sexual abuse using college samples', *Psychological Bulletin*, 124, pp. 22–53

Rind, B. (2001) 'Gay and bisexual adolescent boys' sexual experiences with men: an empirical examination of psychological correlates in a non-clinical sample', *Archives of Sexual Behavior*, 30, pp. 345–68

Risch, N.J., Squires-Wheeler, E. and Keats, B.J.B. (1993) 'Male sexual orientation and genetic evidence', *Science*, 262, pp. 2063–5

Robinson, S.J. and Manning, J.T. (2000) 'The ratio of 2nd to 4th digit length and male homosexuality', *Evolution and Human Behavior*, 21, pp. 333–45

Roselli, C.E., Larkin, K., Resko, J.A., Stellflug, J.N. and Stormshak, F. (2004) 'The volume of a sexually dimorphic nucleus in the ovine medial preoptic area/anterior hypothalamus varies with sexual partner preference. *Endocrinology*, 145, pp. 478–83

Rosen, R.C. and Beck, J.G. (1988) *Patterns of Sexual Arousal: Psychophysiological Processes and Clinical Applications*, New York, NY: Guildford

Ruble, D.N. and Martin, C.L. (1998) 'Gender development', in Damon, W. and Eisenberg, N. (eds), *Handbook of Child Psychology: Social, Emotional and Personality Development*, 5th edn, Vol. 3. New York, NY: Wiley

Saifi, G.M. and Chandra, H.S. (1999) 'An apparent excess of sex and reproduction related genes on the human X chromosome', *Proceedings of the Royal Society of London, Series B: Biological Sciences*, 266, pp. 203–9

Sakheim, D.K., Barlow, D.H., Beck, J.G. and Abrahamson, D.J. (1985) 'A comparison of male heterosexual and male homosexual patterns of sexual arousal', *Journal of Sex Research*, 21, pp. 183–98

Salais, D. and Fischer, R.B. (1995) 'Sexual preference and altruism', *Journal of Homosexuality*, 28, pp. 185–96

Sanders, A.R. *et al.* (1998) 'Poster presentation 149', annual meeting of the American Psychiatric Association, Toronto, Canada

Sanders, G. and Ross-Field, L. (1986) 'Sexual orientation and visuo-spatial ability', *Brain and Cognition*, 5, pp. 280–90

Sanders, G. and Wright, M. (1997) 'Sexual orientation differences in cerebral asymmetry and in the performance of sexually dimorphic cognitive and motor tasks', *Archives of Sexual Behavior*, 26, pp. 463–80

Scamvougeras, A., Witelson, S.F., Branskill, M., Stanchev, P., Black, S., Cheung, G., Steiner, M. and Buck, B. (1994) 'Sexual orientation and anatomy of the corpus callosum', *Society for Neuroscience Abstracts*, 20, pp. 1425

Schmidt, G. and Clement, U. (1995) 'Does peace prevent homosexuality?', *Journal of Homosexuality*, 28, pp. 269–75

Schofield, M. (1965) *Sociological Aspects of Homosexuality*, London: Longmans Green

Silverman, I., Kastuk, D., Choi, J. and Phillips, K. (1999) 'Testosterone levels and spatial ability in men', *Psychoneuroendocrinology*, 24, pp. 813–22

Singh, D., Vidaurri, M., Zambarano, R.J. and Dabbs, J.M. (1999) 'Lesbian erotic role identification: behavioral, morphological and hormonal correlates', *Journal of Personality and Social Psychology*, 76, pp. 1035–49

Singh, J. and Verma, I.C. (1987) 'Influence of major histo(in)compatibility complex on reproduction', *American Journal of Reproductive Immunology and Microbiology*, 15, pp. 150–52

Slabbekoorn, D., Van Goozen, S.H.M., Sanders, G., Gooren, L.T.G. and Cohen-Kettenis, P.T. (2000) 'The dermatoglyphic characteristics of transsexuals: is there evidence for an organising effect of sexual hormones?', *Psychoneuroendocrinology*, 25, pp. 365–75

Slater, E. (1962) 'Birth order and maternal age of homosexuals', *The Lancet*, 1, pp. 69–71

Spitzer, R.L. (2003) 'Can some gay men and lesbians change their sexual orientation? 200 participants report a change from homosexual to heterosexual orientation', *Archives of Sexual Behavior*, 32, pp. 403–17

Sprecher, S., Sullivan, Q. and Hatfield, E. (1994) 'Mate selection preferences: gender differences examined in a national sample', *Journal of Personality and Social Psychology*, 66, pp. 1074–80

Strong, S.M., Singh, D. and Randall, P.K. (2000) 'Childhood gender nonconformity and body dissatisfaction in gay and heterosexual men', *Sex Roles*, 43, 427–39

Sulloway, F.J. (1996) *Born to Rebel: Birth Order, Family Dynamics and Creative Lives*, New York, NY: Pantheon

Swaab, D.F. and Hofman, M.A. (1990) 'An enlarged suprachiasmatic nucleus in homosexual men', *Brain Research*, 537, pp. 141–8

Swaab, D.F., Slob, A.K., Houtsmuller, E.J., Bran, T. and Zhou, J.N. (1995) 'Increased number of vasopressin neurons in the suprachiasmatic nucleus (SCN) of "bisexual" adult male rats following perinatal treatment with aromatase blocker ATD', *Brain Research*, 85, pp. 273–9

Sykes, B. (2003) *Adam's Curse*, New York, NY: Bantam

Symons, D. (1979) *The Evolution of Human Sexuality*, New York, NY: Oxford University Press

Tasker, F. and Golombok, S. (1997) *Growing Up in a Lesbian Family*, New York, NY: Guildford Press

Taylor, T. (1997) *The Prehistory of Sex*, London: Fourth Estate

Tenhula, W.N. and Bailey, J.M (1998) 'Female sexual orientation and pubertal onset', *Developmental Neuropsychology*, 14, pp. 369–83

Tortorice, J. (2001) 'Gender identity, sexual orientation and second-to-fourth digit ratio in females', *Human Behavior and Evolution Society Abstracts*, 13, 35

Traeen, B., Stigum, H. and Sorensen, D. (2002) 'Sexual diversity among urban Norwegians', *Journal of Sex Research*, 39, pp. 249–58

Trivers, R.L. (1974) 'Parent–offspring conflict', *American Zoologist*, 14, pp. 249–64

Turner, W.J. (1995) 'Homosexuality, Type 1: an Xq28 phenomenon', *Archives of Sexual Behavior*, 24, pp. 109–34

Vasey, P.L. (1995) 'Homosexual behavior in primates: a review of evidence and theory', *International Journal of Primatology*, 16, pp. 173–204

Vates, T.S., Fleming, P., Leleszi, J.P., Barthold, J.S., Gonzalez, R. and Perlmutter, A.D. (1999) 'Functional, social and psychosexual adjustment after vaginal reconstruction', *Journal of Urology*, 162, pp. 182–7

Vernier, M.C. (1975) 'Sex differential placentation immunological interactions between male conceptus and gravida during normal pregnancy', *Biology of the Neonate*, 26, pp. 76–87

Ward, I.L. (1972) 'Prenatal stress feminizes and demasculinizes the behavior of males', *Science*, 143, pp. 212–18

Ward, O.B., Ward, I.L., Denning, J.H., Hendricks, S.E. and French, J.A. (2002) 'Hormonal mechanisms underlying aberrant sexual differentiation in male rats prenatally exposed to alcohol, stress, or both', *Archives of Sexual Behavior*, 31, pp. 9–16

Wegesin, D.J. (1998a) 'A neuropsychologic profile of homosexual and heterosexual men and women', *Archives of Sexual Behavior*, 27, pp. 91–108

Wegesin, D.J. (1998b) 'Relation between language lateralisation and spatial ability in gay and straight men and women', *Laterality*, 3, pp. 227–39

Wegesin, D.J. (1998c) 'Event related potentials in homosexual and heterosexual men and women: sex dimorphic patterns in verbal asymmetries and mental rotations', *Brain and Cognition*, 36, pp. 73–92

Weinrich, J.D., Grant, I., Jacobson, D.L., Robinson, S.R. and McCutchan, J.A. (1992) 'Effects of recalled childhood gender nonconformity on adult genitor-erotic role and AIDS exposure', *Archives of Sexual Behavior*, 21, pp. 559–85

Wellings, K., Field, J., Johnson, A.M. and Wadsworth, J. (1994) *Sexual Behaviour in Britain: The National Survey of Sexual Attitudes and Lifestyles*, Harmondsworth: Penguin

Whitam, F.L. (1983) 'Culturally invariable properties of male homosexuality: tentative conclusions from cross-cultural research', *Archives of Sexual Behavior*, 12, pp. 207–26

Whitam, F.L., Daskalos, C., Sobolewski, C.G. and Padilla, P. (1998) 'The emergence of lesbian sexuality and identity cross-culturally: Brazil, Peru, the Philippines, and the United States', *Archives of Sexual Behavior*, 27, pp. 31–56

Whitam, F.L., Diamond, M. and Martin, J. (1993) 'Homosexual orientation in twins: a report on 61 pairs and 3 triplet sets', *Archives of Sexual Behavior*, 22, pp. 187–206

Whitam, F.L. and Mathy, R.M. (1991) 'Childhood cross-gender behavior of homosexual females in Brazil, Peru, the Philippines, and the United States', *Archives of Sexual Behavior*, 20, pp. 151–70

Whitam, F.L. and Zent, M. (1984) 'A cross-cultural assessment of early cross-gender behavior and familial factors in male homosexuality', *Archives of Sexual Behavior*, 13, pp. 427–39

Williams, T.J., Pepitone, M.E., Christensen, S.E., Cooke, B.M., Huberman, A.D., Breedlove, N.J., Breedlove, T.J., Jordan, C.L. and Breedlove, S.M. (2000) 'Finger-length ratio and sexual orientation', *Nature*, 404, pp. 455–6

Wilson, E.O. (1975) *Sociobiology: The New Synthesis*, Cambridge, MA: Belknap

Wilson, E.O. (1978) *On Human Nature*, Cambridge, MA: Harvard University Press

Wilson, G.D. (1983) 'Finger-length as an index of assertiveness in women', *Personality and Individual Differences*, 4, pp. 111–12

Wisniewski, A.B., Migeon, C.J., Meyer-Bahlburg, H.F.L., Gearhart, J.P., Berkovitz, G.D., Brown, T.R. and Money, J. (2000) 'Complete androgen insensitivity syndrome: long term medical, surgical and psychosexual outcome', *Journal of Clinical Endocrinology and Metabolism*, 85, pp. 2664–9

Witelson, S.F. (1989) 'Hand and sex differences in the isthmus and genu of the human corpus callosum', *Brain*, 112, pp. 799–835

Witelson, S.F. and Goldsmith, C.H. (1991) 'The relationship of hand preference to anatomy of the corpus callosum in men', *Brain Research*, 545, pp. 175–182

Zucker, K.J., Bradley, S.J., Oliver, G., Blake, J., Fleming, S. and Hood, J. (1996) 'Psychosexual development of women with congenital adrenal hyperplasia', *Hormones and Behavior*, 30, pp. 300–18

Zucker, K.J., Green, R., Coates, S., Zuger, B., Cohen-Kettenis, P.T., Zecca, G.M., Lertora, V., Money, J., Hahn-Burke, S., Bradley, S.J. and Blanchard, R. (1997) 'Sibling sex ratio of boys with gender identity disorder', *Journal of Child Psychology and Psychiatry*, 38, pp. 543–51

Zuckerman, F. and Head, J.R. (1985) 'Susceptibility of mouse trophoblast to antibody and complement-mediated damage', *Transplantation Proceedings*, 17, pp. 925–7

INDEX

5-alpha-reductase pathway, 70–1

absent father hypothesis, 32
Adams, H.E, 15
adaptive value of homosexuality, 57–67
adoption studies, 45
arginine vasopressin neurons (AVP),
    111
Alexander, Joel E., 122
alienation theory (Bem), 38–9
Allen, Laura S., 110, 124
alpha activity, 122
Ames, M.A., 69–70
Ancient Greeks, 23–4
androgen insensitivity syndrome (AIS),
    76, 78, 131
androgen receptors, 55, 70, 76, 113
Angst, J., 100
animal models, 62–3
anterior commissure (AC), 124–5
aromatase pathway 70–1, 111, 114
auditory evoked potentials (AEPs), 83–4

Bagemihl, B., 62–3
Bailey, J. Michael, 19, 21, 36, 38, 44,
    47–9, 51, 58, 60–1, 65, 72, 88, 90,
    91, 128–9, 138, 147
Baker, R.R., 61
Bakker, J., 114
balanced polymorphism, 59–61
Baum, M.J., 109
Baumeister, R.F., 27, 39

Bauserman, R., 35
Beck, J.G., 39
behavioural genetics, 45–52, 130
Bell, A.P., 57, 139
Bellis, M.A., 61
Bem, Daryl, J., 38–9, 100–1
Benishay, B.A., 44
Berenbaum, S.A., 130
big brother effect, 39, 79, 95–103
bimodality, 16–22
birth weight, 102, 104
bisexuality, 14–21
Blanchard, Ray, 32, 39, 86, 88, 96–9,
    102–5, 131
blank slate notion, 29
Bobrow, D., 58
Bogaert, A.F., 85–6, 88, 97–101, 103
bonding, same-sex, 61–2
Bonobos, 63
Bradley, S.J., 73
brain
    asymmetry, 121–2
    auditory processing, 82–4
    gay–straight differences, 107–26
    plasticity of, 39, 41
    regions involved in cognitive abilities,
        120
    responses to erotica, 15
    sexual differentiation of, 104, 109
Brown, W.M., 78, 142
Buhrich, N., 32
Byne, W., 110, 112–13

Callow, Simon, 14
Cameron, K., 34
Cameron, P., 34
Campbell, Anne, 65
Cantor, James M., 99
castration anxiety, 31
Celotti, F., 125
Champlin, C.A., 84
Chandra, H.S., 54
childhood gender non-conformity
    (CGN), 39, 49, 92, 130–3, 139
child-rearing effects, 29, 36–8,
Chivers, M.L., 21
Clark, M.M., 84
'Clause 28', 34, 148
Clement, U., 90
cognitive ability profiles, 116–21
Cole-Harding, S., 91
conditioning, 33–4
Condy, S., 35
congenital adrenal hyperplasia (CAH),
    74–6
contagion theory, 33–6, 101
Cooke, B.M., 114
Copas, A.J., 25
Copeland, P., 57
Corliss, H.L., 133
corpus callosum (CC), 125
Cowell, P.E., 125
cross-cultural comparisons, 23, 38

Dancey, C.P., 71, 140–1
Davis, E.C., 109
Dawood, Khytam, 34–5, 49
definition of homosexuality, 13
dermatoglyphics, 80–2
developmental instability, 92–4, 147
Diamond, L.M., 26
Diamond, M., 73
dichotic listening tests, 121–2
Dickson, N., 18, 25
diethylstilbestrol (DES), 75–6

differential reinforcement theory, 37
dihydrotestosterone (DHT), 70, 74, 80
Dittman, R.W., 75
Dorner, Gunter, 90
drug use, maternal, 91–2
Dunn, Judy, 100
DuPree, M.G., 55

Ehrhardt, A.A., 73, 76
Electra complex, 31
electroencephalography (EEG), 122–3
Ellis, Lee, 69–70, 91, 102
Erens, B., 17, 24
Ernst, C., 100
Estep, K.W., 61
Everitt, B.J., 39
evolutionary theory, 57–67
Eysenck, H.J., 33

falsifiability, as criterion of scientific
    theory, 32
familiality, 43–5
Feeney, J.A., 32
Fernandez-Gausti, A., 70, 113–14
Finegan, J.K., 131–32
finger-length ratios, 77–80, 93, 142–3
fingerprints, 80–2
Fischer, R.B., 58, 61
fluctuating asymmetry, 93
fluoxetine, 112–13
foetal development, 69–70, 89–94, 125
Forastieri, V., 81–2
fraternal birth order, 95–106
Freud, Sigmund, 30–3, 46
Freund, K., 21, 32, 85
Friesen, C., 86, 88

Galaburda, A.M., 122
Gangestad, S.W., 26
Gearhart, J.P., 74
gender reassignment, 73–4, 130
gender identity 130–4

genetic factors, 43–56, 130
genital measures, 15, 20–2
Geshchwind, N., 124
Getz, W.M., 64
Gladue, B.A., 61, 118
Goldsmith, C.H., 125
Golombok, Susan, 37
Gorski, R.A., 109–10, 124
Goy, R.W., 72
Green, R., 93, 97, 105, 129
Greenberg, A.S., 147
Grimshaw, G.M., 118, 132
growth measures, 86–8
Gualtieri, T., 104
Habib, M., 125

Hall, J.A.Y., 82, 118–19
Hamer, Dean, H., 19–20, 25, 44, 50–3, 55, 57, 61, 146
handedness, 41–2, 63, 93, 123–5, 149
Harris, J.R., 29
Head, J.R., 104
Hellberg, J., 91
Helle, S., 103
Heller, W., 122
Herdt, G., 38
Herman, R.A., 85
Herschberger, S., 38, 85, 133
Hicks, R.E., 104
Hines, Melanie, 92, 130–1
Hiscock, M., 122
Hofman, M.A., 111
Homeobox genes, 78
homophobia, 15, 21, 27
Houtsmuller, E.J., 109
Howard, R.C., 39
hormones
    and butch–femme distinction, 140–2
    and growth, 86–8
    and pubertal onset, 88–9
    and spatial ability, 119

organizational vs activational effects, 71
    prenatal, 54–6, 65, 69–94
Hu, S., 52
Hudson, Rock, 14
H-Y antigen, 103–6
hypothalamus, 70, 89, 107–15

inclusive fitness, 57–9
intersexual conditions, 72–6
interstitial nucleus of anterior hypothalamus (INAH), 110–14
Isay, R.A., 32
Islamic views, 14

Jamison, C.S., 81
Johnson, A.M., 17, 23–4
Jones, M.B., 97
Jung, Carl, 31

Kallmann, Franz J., 46–7
Karama, S., 112
Kendler, Kenneth S., 49
Kimura, Doreen, 82, 118–19
kin selection, 57–9
Kindon, H.A., 109
Kinnunen, Leann H., 112–13
Kinsey, Alfred C., 16–22, 25, 45, 48
Kinsey scales, 16–22, 25
Kirk, K.M., 45
Kirkpatrick, R.C., 61, 64
Klassen, P., 104
Krujiver, F.P.M., 113

Lalumiere, M.L., 92–3, 124, 126
Lasco, M.S., 125
Laumann, E.O., 17, 100–1
lesbianism
    adaptive value, 65
    and finger lengths, 79–80
    and the limbic system, 115
    and handedness, 124

butch–femme types, 71, 137–44
cognitive abilities, 119
in CAH women, 75
in DES women, 76
prevalence of, 13–37
lesbian mothers, 37
LeVay, Simon, 9, 16–17, 19, 110, 112–13, 146, 147
Levy, J., 122
Liberace, 14
Lippa, Richard A., 37, 79, 132–3
Little Britain (television programme), 23
Loulan, J., 139
Lutchmaya, S., 78

Macke, Jennifer P., 55, 113
Malcolm, J., 51, 66
Manning, J.T., 77–9
Martensen-Larsen, O., 96
Martin, C.L., 37
Martin, J.T., 87
McConaghy, N., 32
McCormick, C.M., 118, 122
McEwen, B.S., 131
McFadden, D., 79–80, 82–5, 115, 126
McKnight, J., 51, 59, 60, 65–6
magnetoencephalography, 123
maternal line effects, 50–3, 66
maternal drug use, 91–2
maternal immune system, 102–6
maternal stress, 89–92
Mathy, R.M., 130
Meaney, M.J., 131
menstrual cycle, 71
Meyer-Bahlburg, H.F.L., 71, 76
Mikach, S.M., 65
Miller, E.M., 60, 65
mitochondrial DNA, 53–4
Moffat, S.D., 125
Moller, A.P., 92
Money, John, 14, 73, 75
mosaic brain, 11

Muscarella, Frank, 61, 64
Mustanski, B.S., 82, 93

Neave, N., 71, 118–19, 125
Nedoma, K., 85
Nguyen, D.H., 87
Nyborg, Helmut, 118

Oedipus complex, 31–2
oestrogen receptors, 114
otoacoustic emissions (OEAs), 82–4

Paredes, R.G., 109
parental manipulation, 59
Pasanen, E.G., 82–3
Pattatucci, A.M.L., 25, 44, 51–2, 61
Patterson, C., 37
Pavlov, Ivan, 33
Pearcey, S.M., 140
Pellis, S.M., 131
penile plethysmograph, 20–2
penis envy, 31–2
penis size, 84–5
Peplau, L.A., 39
Perkins, M.W., 140
Perret, D.I., 60
Phoenix, C.H., 72
Pillard, Richard C., 43–4, 47
Pinker, Steven, 29, 41, 55
Plomin, Robert, 100
Poasa, K.H., 97
prenatal androgen theory, 69–94
pre-pulse inhibition of startle reflex (PPI), 115
prevalence of homosexuality, 22–4
psychoanalysis, 30–3
psychobiology, 10
psychosocial theories, 29–42, 59, 100–2
puberty, onset of, 88–9
Purcell, D.W., 97

Rahman, Qazi, 64, 79, 93, 111, 115, 118–20, 143
recruitment bias, 36, 40–1, 48
Reiner, W.G., 74
Reite, Martin, 122
reparative therapy, 40–2
Rhesus blood factor, 103
Rhodes, G., 60
Rice, George, 52
Rice, W.R., 64
Ridge, S.R., 32
Rieger, G., 21
Rind, B., 35
Risch, N.J., 51
Robinson, S.J., 79
Roselli, C.E., 114
Rosen, R.C., 39
Ross-Field, L., 118, 122
Ruble, D.N., 37

Saifi, G.M., 54
Sakheim, D.K., 21
Salais, D., 58, 61
Sambia tribe, 38
Sanders, A.R., 51
Sanders, G., 118, 122
Scamvougeras, A., 125
Schofield, M., 96
Schubel, E,. 79–80
seduction hypothesis, 34–6, 101
self-labelling of sex orientation, 14
sexually antagonistic selection, 64
sexually dimorphic nucleus (SDN), 109, 114
Sigmundson, H.K., 73
Silber, K., 111
Silverman, I., 119
Singh, Devendra, 141–3
sissy-boy syndrome, 39, 127–30
Skinner, B.F., 33
Skyscraper Test, 14
Slabbekoorn, D., 82

Slater, E., 96
sleep–wake cycle, 111
Slob, A.K., 114
Snyder, E., 130
social learning theory, 33–4
Spitzer, Robert, L., 40–1
stability of sex orientation, 23–5
stress, prenatal, 89–92
Sufka, Kenneth J., 122
Sulloway, F.J., 100–2
supra-chiasmatic nucleus (SCN), 110–11
Swaab, D.F., 110–11
Swaddle, J.P., 92
Sykes, Bryan, 53–4
Symons, Donald, 60

Tan, F.D., 133
Tasker, Fiona, 37
taxometry, 26
Taylor, T., 23
Tenhula, W.N., 88
therapy
    aversion, 40, 150
    for sexuality, 40–2, 134,
tomboy behaviour, 39, 127–33
Tortorice, J., 142
Traeen, B., 19
Trivers, R.L., 59
twin research, 38, 45–9, 130
Turner, W.J., 66

vaginal photoplethysmography, 20–2
Vasey, Paul L., 62–3
Vates, T.S., 74
Verma, I.C., 104
Vernier, M.C., 104

waist–hip ratio, 141
Ward, I.L., 90
Ward, O.B., 90
Watson, J.B., 33

...ley, 118–19, 122–3
Weinberg, M., 57
Weinrich, James D., 43–4, 134, 139
Wellings, K., 17, 24, 34
Whitham, Frederick L., 23, 47, 130
Williams, T.J., 78–9
Wilde, Oscar, 14
Wilson, Edward O., 57–8
Wilson, Glenn D., 33, 57, 64, 78–9, 93, 115, 118–20
Wisniewski, A.B., 76

Witelson, Sandra F., 118, 122, 125
Wright, M., 122

X-linkage, 50–6, 66

Young, R., 93

Zent, M., 130
Zucker, Kenneth J., 75, 128, 130
Zuckerman, F., 104